9.20

The Lure of God

LEWIS S. FORD

THE LURE OF GOD

A Biblical Background for Process Theism

FORTRESS PRESS   PHILADELPHIA

Library of Congress Cataloging in Publication Data

Ford, Lewis S
  The lure of God.

  Includes bibliographical references and indexes.
    1. Process theology.   2. Bible–Theology.   I. Title.
  BT83.6.F67   230   77-15230
  ISBN 0-8006-0516-0

6521L77   Printed in the United States of America   1-516

For
Stephanie and Rachel

Contents

Preface

In recent years, since the "death of God" movement heralded the collapse of neo-orthodoxy, process theism has become a viable alternative for the contemporary appropriation of the Christian faith for an increasing number of people.Theologians are recognizing the need for a wider conceptuality which frees theology from the ghetto of sacred history and places it within the whole sweep of human and natural history. Process thought, reflecting upon the mutual interaction among God, humanity, and natural actualities, conveys a sense of ecological balance between both nature and God. This challenges many of the presuppositions of classical theism by overcoming their felt conflicts and contradictions.

Yet much of what has been written as "process theology" is really simply philosophy written within the context of a Christian perspective. It is a sustained reflection upon the generic features of experience, taking seriously those dimensions of experience most fully apparent within the religious life. This sense of Christian philosophizing has been carefully articulated by John B. Cobb, Jr., in the final chapter of *A Christian Natural Theology.*[1] In times past, from the Middle Ages down to Hegel and Kierkegaard, most philosophizing was written from within the Christian tradition, however much it sought to emancipate itself from the church. This, in turn, dictated much of the theologian's apologetic method. He ferreted out these implicit Christian elements in the reigning philosophies and related them to the more historically conditioned symbols of the church's faith. More and more, however, philosophy's attempt to become radically secular, divorcing itself from all ties with Christian theism, has become successful, leaving fewer avenues of approach open to the theologian. As a result the theologian is forced to become his own philosopher. This need not interfere with the rigor he brings to the task, provided his speculative thinking subjects itself to the recognized philosophical canons. His theory must be both consistent and coherent in itself, and adequate and applicable to human experience. But it has meant that Christian philosophizing has become less and less the task of the professional philosopher and has been relegated more and more to the theologian.

This task of Christian philosophizing is well worth doing, and we should be grateful to the many process theologians who have been willing to devote themselves to this end. As a result, however, the distinctively theological task has been comparatively neglected. This study seeks to redress the balance. While using a conceptuality largely framed by process philosophy, it addresses for the most part the historically contingent elements within the Christian tradition: the biblical witness to Israel and to Jesus, his role as the Christ, the meaning of his death and resurrection, and the implications of the Christian proclamation of the Trinity.

Oftentimes traditional theism has seen itself as the legitimate heir of the biblical faith. Process theologians are then cast in the role of radical, even iconoclastic, innovators. I wish to indicate those aspects of the biblical tradition that have been suppressed by this reigning orthodoxy, and to show that process theism has as good (or even better) a purchase on this tradition as classical theism.

Process philosophy is a convenient label designating the thought of Alfred North Whitehead and his intellectual associate Charles Hartshorne. For theological purposes, Hartshorne is clearly the more accessible, and most, including myself, have been introduced to process theology through his wise tutelage. Nevertheless, there are subtle but important differences between them, and where they differ I find myself siding with Whitehead.[2] Since Whitehead's conceptuality is presupposed in my extensions and applications, it seemed best to introduce the reader to this thought by way of an intellectual biography tracing the development of his theism. Thus those unfamiliar with Whitehead or Hartshorne's philosophy can feel at home with this book. While it delves into some of the intricacies involved in applying Whitehead's thought to basic Christian doctrines, it addresses the general reader, explaining these Whiteheadian categories as they are needed for this task.

Although this is properly an essay in Christian theology, my professional background lies in philosophy and, to a lesser extent, in biblical studies. This may be an unorthodox preparation for theology, but I am persuaded that it is a necessary one in this day and age. Too much theologizing is based merely upon the pale reflection of itself which it sees in philosophy, and needs a more thorough grounding in biblical studies. On the other hand, theology is often insufficiently rigorous philosophically. Philosophy and biblical studies are the two extremes which need to be fruitfully married in the theological enterprise. Whether this marriage is successful or not must be left to the reader to decide.

While this essay has been planned as a continuous whole with its own integrity, portions of individual chapters have appeared elsewhere. Two were originally presented as lectures: chapter one was presented at the Moravian Theological Seminary, Bethlehem, Pennsylvania, on February 14, 1974; chapter three was given at the Conference on Biblical Theology and Process Philosophy at the Christian Theological Seminary, Indianapolis, Indiana, on March 1, 1974. An earlier version of chapter two appeared in *Interpretation* 26/2 (April 1972), 198–209, while chapter four has drawn on materials originally appearing in "Lionel S. Thornton and Process Christology," *Anglican Theological Review* 55/4 (October 1973), 479–83; "The Incarnation as a Contingent Reality: A Reply to Dr. Pailin," *Religious Studies* 8/2 (June 1972), 169–73; "The Possibilities for Process Christology," *Encounter* 35/4 (Winter 1974), 281–94; and "Theological Reflections on Extra-Terrestrial Life," originally given as the Faculty Research Lecture for the Spring of 1968 at Raymond College of the University of the Pacific, Stockton, California, and published in *The Raymond Review* 2/2 (Fall 1968), 1–14. Most of chapter five appeared in *Religion in Life* 42/4 (Winter 1973), 466–78; while chapter seven is an abridged and simplified version of "Process Trinitarianism," *Journal of the American Academy of Religion* 43/2 (June 1975), 199–213.

Many friends have helped this endeavor by commenting on individual chapters. To others I am grateful for their comments on the entire manuscript: particularly Delwin Brown, Dwayne Cole, Bernard Lee, Marjorie Suchocki, Andrew Tunyogi, and Philip Verhalen.

NOTES

1. John B. Cobb, Jr., *A Christian Natural Theology* (Philadelphia: Westminster Press, 1965).
2. See the monograph I edited, *Two Process Philosophers: Hartshorne's Encounter with Whitehead* (American Academy of Religion: AAR Studies in Religion 5, 1973).

Abbreviations

AI   Alfred North Whitehead, *Adventures of Ideas* (New York: Macmillan, 1933)

CPA   John B. Cobb, Jr., *Christ in a Pluralistic Age* (Philadelphia: Westminster Press, 1975)

IL   Lionel S. Thornton, *The Incarnate Lord* (London: Longmans, Green, 1928)

PC   David R. Griffin, *A Process Christology* (Philadelphia: Westminster Press, 1973)

PR   Alfred North Whitehead, *Process and Reality* (New York: Macmillan, 1929)

RM   Alfred North Whitehead, *Religion in the Making* (New York: Macmillan, 1926)

SMW   Alfred North Whitehead, *Science and the Modern World* (New York: Macmillan, 1926), second edition

CHAPTER 1

Whitehead's Pilgrimage to Process Theism

In this book we shall be considering how the particular conceptuality of process theism can illuminate our understanding of biblical and Christian traditions. By process theism we largely mean the particular conception of God which the mathematician Alfred North Whitehead fashioned in later life. The understanding of God that he came to is sharply critical of many of our inherited notions, particularly concerning divine omniscience, omnipotence, and immutability. Whitehead's thought suggests ways we might free ourselves from the problems and difficulties that have burdened theology for centuries, and even allows us some dimensions of the biblical message which we have neglected and have not really appreciated.

Before we embark on a theological appropriation of process theism, however, it will be instructive to see how Whitehead himself came to espouse it. He once wrote: "Aristotle found it necessary to complete his metaphysics by the introduction of a Prime Mover—God.... in his consideration of this metaphysical question he was entirely dispassionate; and he is the last European metaphysician of first-rate importance for whom this claim can be made. After Aristotle, ethical and religious interests began to influence metaphysical conclusions."[1] This same claim can be made in Whitehead's case: he came to incorporate the existence of God within his system largely by philosophical reflections on the problem. William Ernest Hocking, one of Whitehead's Harvard colleagues, reports that, concerning the idea of God, Whitehead told him, "I should never have included it, if it had not been strictly required for descriptive completeness. You must set all your essentials into the foundation. It's no use putting up a set of terms, and then remarking, 'Oh, by the by, I believe there's a God.'"[2]

Whitehead was born in 1861, two years after Darwin's *Origin of the Species* was published, on the Isle of Thanet, the easternmost tip of southern England. His father was an Anglican clergyman of the evangelical school. Whitehead studied at Sherborne which, while he was a student there, celebrated its thousandth anniversary. It had begun as a Benedictine monastery and then later became, under Edward VI, one of the public schools of England. During his senior year he lived in what was thought to have been the abbot's cell, and became steeped in Anglican piety and tradition. Then he went up to Cambridge. Professionally, Whitehead studied and taught only mathematics at Trinity College, Cambridge during his years there, from 1880 to 1910. As an undergraduate he talked openly and freely about his interest in religion, especially about foreign missions. "We may not know precisely what many of Jesus' sayings mean," he is reported to have said, "but the commandment to go into all the world and preach the gospel is very clear."[3]

Bertrand Russell reports that at one point "as a young man, he was almost converted to Roman Catholicism under the influence of Cardinal Newman."[4] However, these early convictions faded and Whitehead became doubtful and uncertain. The cause for this may well have been the problem that faced many Victorians, the problem of God's omnipotence and the presence of evil in the world. If God is all-powerful then he must be negligent in doing anything about evil. So Whitehead decided to take up the study of theology. Lucien Price records: "This study went on for years, eight of them, I think he said. When he had finished with the subject, for he had finished with it, he called in a Cambridge bookseller and asked him what he would give for the lot."[5] He gave up the subject, sold all the books, and gave up on theology. The theologians failed to persuade him. Russell confirms this: "Throughout the time that I knew him well—that is to say, roughly, from 1898 to 1912—he was very definitely and emphatically agnostic."[6]

During all these years a revolution was occurring in physics. With the advent of Einstein's relativity theories, both special and general, the foundations of physics to which Whitehead had grown accustomed were completely shattered. He belonged to the generation that really was convinced that physics was on a firm foundation, that practically everything in the discipline had been discovered. Its principles were set; they had been that way ever since the time of Newton—and would remain that way. Now the whole theory was up for grabs. He said he was fooled once about the certainty of the foundation of physics and he was sure he would not be fooled again. Thus Whitehead's thinking thereafter always had an element of tentativeness; he was painfully aware of the difficulties in discovering the final foundations of things.

He then undertook a series of studies on the foundations of natural science: *An Inquiry into the Principles of Natural Knowledge* (1919), *The Concept of Nature* (1920), and *The Principle of Relativity* (1922). The last book is a critique of Einstein's theory of relativity, proposing a comparable theory to put in its place. It has not received much of a hearing principally because his objections to Einstein are primarily philosophical. The book is written in three parts—a philosophical intro-duction, a section on physics, and a section on mathematics, requiring expertise in all three areas. I doubt if many readers have really understood the work.

In the meantime, after thirty years at Cambridge, Whitehead pulled up stakes and moved to London. Eventually he became Dean of the Faculty of Science at the Imperial College of Science and Technology, and was very heavily involved in administration. As he was approaching retire-ment, after a lifetime of teaching mathematics, with publications in mathematics, the philosophy of nature, and logic, he was offered a chair in philosophy at Harvard. It was in this country that his metaphysics, and with it his philosophical theism, developed.

His first metaphysical synthesis was presented in the Lowell Lectures of February 1925, later incorporated in *Science and the Modern World*. These lectures are largely consonant with the philosophy of events that Whitehead had already developed in his philosophy of nature. These replaced the traditional elements of space, time, and matter with spatiotemporal volumes (events) having certain characteristics (objects). In this view we may conceive of anything material as a series of events having persistent characteristics that are constantly exemplified over a period of time. The material object is simply an expression of the stability and persistence of these characteristics exemplified in the events. Such events express the static repetition of the past, whereas any dynamic activity constitutes an ever-changing series of events.

These Lowell Lectures polemicize against the prevailing scientific materialism inherited from the seventeenth century, and propose an alternative "philosophy of organism" based upon events and objects ordered in terms of organic mechanism. Although the lectures examine the interaction of science and religion, they are quite neutral with respect to the existence of God. Yet when he came to publish these lectures in June of that same year, he included several additions, among which was a chapter on "God," arguing for God's existence and describing his nature as Whitehead then conceived it. We must scrutinize these additions very closely for clues they might give to the development of his philosophical theism.

In his earlier philosophy of nature, and in the original Lowell Lectures, Whitehead conceived of actual events as being divisible into smaller events *ad infinitum*. However, in a section appended to his lecture on "Relativity," Whitehead changed his mind.[7] On this atomic theory of events, there was a lowest threshold for actual events, below which it cannot be subdivided into smaller actual events. We are familiar with this in terms of atomic theories of matter in which it is argued that elementary particles cannot be actually subdivided, although they are extensive and hence mathematically (or potentially) divisible. Whitehead applied this argument, not to material particles but to events, atomic events which he henceforth called "actual occasions."

This has certain implications, such as the denial of determinism. The way the past persists into the present is the essence of efficient causation, and observes the regularity of scientific law. Scientific explanation seeks to account for the present event insofar as it can be understood in terms of its causal antecedents. The ideal of complete explanation, coupled with the assumption that only efficient causation is effective, necessarily yields causal determinism, a methodological postulate widespread among the more hardheaded practitioners of the social sciences, though now less prevalent among natural scientists, especially physicists. I find nothing to object to the ideal of complete explanation, even though it is unrealizable in practice, but I do question this exclusive attention to efficient causation.

Causal determinism follows naturally enough, to be sure, from our ordinary notion that the cause produces its effect. Here productive activity is vested in the antecedent cause, and its effect is merely a passive outcome. But if the event is atomic, it requires a lapse of time in order to become the event which it is. It does not instantaneously arise out of its antecedent causes. Yet, if these totally determine it, it should. This may well be a possible anticipation of Heisenberg's uncertainty principle, that the past conditions for any event only determine its outcome within certain parameters. Below those parameters the physicist sees only random action, that is, a determination not caused by the past conditions.

A second implication involves a reversal of our ordinary understanding that causes produce effects. The cause must precede its effect in time, yet it must be presently existent in order to be active in producing its effect. If, however, temporal atomicity requires a lapse of time in order to bring the effect into being, its causes are already past and gone before the effect arises. This generates a contradiction: the cause must precede the effect in order to be its cause, yet if it precedes the effect by any lapse of time, the cause can no longer be active or effective in producing the effect. The usual theory managed to bridge this gap by claiming that the cause is instantaneous with its effect, thus it is present with the effect while at the same time it precedes the effect. But if there is a lapse of time, then the cause is past and gone. Whitehead challenged customary thinking by reasoning that it is the event in the present that should be taken to be active. Instead of an active cause producing a passive effect, he argues that there is a present event producing itself out of its passive past causes.

We do have a model we might adopt for this sort of causation, which is perception. In perception the sensory impressions which we receive are objective causes in that they determine the character of what it is that we are perceiving. But the way in which we perceive things, the meaning we attach to them, the way we integrate these sensory impressions into a coherent whole involves, as Kant would say, the spontaneous activity of the mind organizing its sensations. Whitehead suggests that this model of perception can be generalized as our model for understanding all causation. Therefore, he takes the word "apprehension," a conscious taking account of other things, and deletes the prefix "ap-" to give us the word "prehension." Prehension is the opposite of the way we generally conceive causation. Therefore, if A causes B, B prehends A. B is constituted by the way in which it prehends A and all its other past causes.

The use of perception to understand causation means that we are now able to bring into one account both causation and perception. Thereby we can overcome the usual dualism by which causation is regarded as a feature of the realm of matter, while perception is conceived as belonging only to mind. It also involves a transformation of our understanding of subjectivity and objectivity. If all (efficient) causes are past, as past they are also objective. They form the data of prehensions. They suggest that what we mean by subjectivity is simply present immediacy. The shift from object to subject is essentially one of temporal terms: that which is objective is past, and what is subjective is what is immediately present to us.

This means, among other things, that subjectivity has nothing particularly to do with human consciousness or mentality. The reason we regularly associate subjectivity with human awareness and consciousness is that this is the only subjectivity of which we are immediately aware. We only know ourselves subjectively. We infer that other persons also enjoy subjectivity, but this we do not know directly. Whitehead argues that if subjectivity is really another way of talking about the felt sense of present immediacy, as opposed to what is past to us, then this is a feature of all events. All events without exception have their own interiority, their own subjectivity. Therefore the language which we should use to describe the coming into being or the emergence of individual events should be subjectivistic language, purged of its associations with human existence, with consciousness, and with mentality. This is really the project that Whitehead undertakes in his major work, *Process and Reality* (1929).

If one purges the notions of mentality and physicality of their associations with subject and object, one comes to a different understanding of them; at least Whitehead did. He came to hold that what we mean by the physical is simply the repetitive, the reiterated, the habitual. The character of molecules reveals them to be most conservative. They can continue to reiterate the same patterns of existence for billions of years. Mentality, on the other hand, is coordination directed toward novel intensity. Insofar as events differ meaningfully from their past, not simply reiterating that which they have inherited, they display some degree of mentality. As for consciousness, Whitehead is not suggesting that there is any more consciousness in the world than we ordinarily assume. This is basically an empirical matter to determine. But it is not necessary for an entity to have either mentality or consciousness for it to be subjective. All enjoy subjectivity in their present immediacy, with varying degrees of physicality and mentality, depending upon how they repeat, or revise, their inherited past. Only a few have any degree of consciousness.

Now, if events produce themselves out of their causes rather than causes produce events as passive effects, then there is an element of self-production in every event which may be understood in terms of spontaneity and freedom. For there is no necessity that a given set of causes must be unified by the event in exactly the same way in each case. Rather there is an influx of a great many causal factors which the occasion in coming into being uses to unify itself. It makes its own actuality out of these causal factors. Whitehead speaks of decision as the mark of actuality, because the occasion decides or cuts off the alternative possibilities of integrating the past in order to become the one single actuality that it is.

This means that there is a place for purpose and for value in the process of actualization. For if one argues that past causes produce the effect, this purports to be a total explanation. One simply has to exhibit what the past causes are in order to explain the present event. If, on the other hand, the present event creates itself by the way it decides how to unify its past, then it is necessary also to introduce purpose to explain how possibilities influence the process. There are real possibilities as to what that particular event can become. These possibilities are valued in that some are better than others with respect to actualization in this event.

Now, it finally developed in Whitehead's thinking that God is the ultimate source of these possibilities. He provides the possibilities for each event, the values in terms of which it can become what it is. To put this argument another way, we can say that God's role is to provide the origin of the occasion's subjectivity. This is a question, I think, that has been rarely faced by philosophy. Philosophers fail to explain how subjects come into being. For example, in Kant's philosophy there is a great deal of discussion concerning the nature of subjectivity. Every rational being uses certain capacities, the categories and the forms of intuition, by which he experiences and orders the world. Very little is said as to how these come into being. If we take a biological account, somehow our subjectivity or consciousness emerges somewhere around the ages of one and two. We cannot remember back in our subjectivity any further than that. Where this subjectivity comes from is just an inexplicable mystery.

Whitehead was faced with this problem acutely because each event enjoys its own subjectivity. How does it acquire this subjectivity? How does it have the capacity to feel or prehend its various causal data and bring them into unity? Whitehead proposes that it begins with an ideal of what it can become, given its particular circumstances. This ideal is what it receives from God, and it achieves its own actualization by the way in which it fuses together all of its efficient causes by means of this ideal of itself. The event is not determined by God because it is capable of using the past causes it inherits to modify that aim. Nor is it determined by its past because it can also use that aim to modify and to influence the way in which it will appropriate the past. Thus both can be played against one another to secure its own spontaneity or freedom.

This theory is only barely hinted at in *Science and the Modern World,* and receives its first full expression in *Process and Reality.* At first God was conceived merely as the principle of limitation or selection, selecting among the infinity of possibilities which otherwise would become available for each occasion. As such he was one of the formative elements of the world, and not an actuality like the actual occasions enjoying his own subjective immediacy. But, as Whitehead saw it, some such principle of limitation was required.

While God's existence was first philosophically required in the revision of Whitehead's first metaphysical synthesis which he appended to his Lowell Lectures of 1925, it would be presumptuous of us to claim that these reflections first caused Whitehead to become a theist once again. Such personal shifts are gradual, often imperceptible. It is unlikely that he remained the emphatic agnostic that Russell knew after the war. In fact, Russell thinks that the death of Whitehead's younger son, Eric, in air combat in 1918, significantly shifted his views: "The pain of this loss had a great deal to do with turning his thoughts to philosophy and with causing him to seek ways of escaping from belief in a merely mechanistic universe."[8] Some sense of this may be gleaned from the dedication of *The Principles of Natural Knowledge* to Eric's memory: "Killed in action over the Forêt de Gobain giving himself that the city of his vision may not perish. The music of his life was without discord, perfect in its beauty."

Moreover, we must remember that the flower of English manhood, including many whom Whitehead taught at Cambridge and London, also perished in this war. Apart from religion, Whitehead was to write, "human life is a flash of occasional enjoyments lighting up a mass of pain and misery, a bagatelle of transient experience."[9]

"Religion and Science," originally delivered as an address in the

Phillips Brooks House at Harvard on Sunday, April 5, 1925, immediately before his discovery of temporal atomism, gives no hint of the philosophical theism Whitehead came to espouse in his chapter on "God." Yet it shows a very high appreciation for *religion,* defined as "the reaction of human nature to its search for God."[10] "It is the one element in human experience which persistently shows an upward trend. It fades and then recurs. But when it renews its force, it recurs with an added richness and purity of content. The fact of the religious vision, and its history of persistent expansion, is our one ground for optimism."[11] Yet this is the *search* for God, a search whose goal is most elusive. "Religion is the vision of something which stands beyond, behind, and within, the passing flux of immediate things; something which is real, and yet waiting to be realised; something which is a remote possibility, and yet the greatest of present facts; something that gives meaning to all that passes, and yet eludes apprehension; something whose possession is the final good, and yet is beyond all reach; something which is the ultimate ideal, and the hopeless quest."[12]

At the same time, Whitehead notes that "there has been a gradual decay of religious influence in European civilisation."[13] He predicts that "religion will not regain its own power until it can face change in the same spirit as does science."[14] For science, "a clash of doctrines is not a disaster—it is an opportunity."[15] Conflicting theories, often buttressed by fresh evidence, provide the opportunity for the expansion, revision, or qualification of existing theories for their improvement. So likewise the expression of religious principles requires continual development, so as to be hospitable to new sensibilities nourished on this scientific advance. At the time, Whitehead appears to have no such revision of our concept of God to offer, although he was shortly to have one. He seems then to be most sympathetic to the religious quest, perhaps himself participating in it, but relegating it primarily to theological concerns. In any case it did not have any place in philosophy, unless strictly required by its fundamental principles.

The notion of God as the principle of the limitation of possibility was the first version that Whitehead developed as to the nature of God, but this concept was considerably modified over the course of the next three or four years. For example, by March 1926, in *Religion in the Making,* Whitehead had come to the conclusion that God could be conceived either as a principle or as a person. Conceived as a principle, God really is very much like Plato's Form of the Good, that is, the principle of order or value in terms of which all the possibilities are organized. Alternatively, one could conceive of God as a personal being who "thinks on thinking," to use the Aristotelian phrase. That is, Whitehead conceived of God during this period in either Platonic or Aristotelian terms. Ultimately, he argued, it did not make any difference. Therefore, he proposed the questionable thesis that all civilized religions really center around the same basic point, namely, that there is a permanent rightness at the center of things. These religions primarily differ as to whether this is to be described in personalistic language as God, or an impersonal language as Brahman, Nirvana, or Tao.

Insofar as God is conceived as personal, God is alone with himself, thinking his own thoughts, apart from the world. In classical Christianity, Aristotle's ideas were taken over, but characteristically modified. In that tradition, instead of thinking of God as a persuasive power who acts as a kind of lure toward which things move, which was Aristotle's conception, Aquinas and others adopted the understanding that God creates by being the ultimate efficient cause for the world. Thus God knows the world by the way in which he creates it. God becomes the ultimate efficient cause, the primary cause of things, separate from the world with all of its secondary causal processes.

Whitehead, however, remains true to the original Aristotelian conception that God acts in terms of final causes, because God's function is to provide the lures for the individual occasions to actualize. Within two years, however, Whitehead saw that the actuality of God also requires that he be influenced and enriched by the world. One of the reasons he came to this conclusion was his insistence that God ought to exemplify the same principles that other actualities in the world have. As he writes in *Process and Reality*, "God is not to be treated as an exception to all metaphysical principles, invoked to save their collapse. He is their chief exemplification."[16]

A second reason stems from Whitehead's claim that every actual occasion has two different kinds of prehensions. It possesses a set of physical prehensions, the way by which it prehends other past actualities which causally influence it. It also has conceptual prehensions which provide the way by which it is influenced by values, ideals, possibilities, and concepts. It needs the latter in order to be oriented toward the future, and the former in order to be oriented toward the past. So every occasion is seen as the fusion of these two types. Yet God was conceived as a being which had an infinite number of prehensions of ideals, possibilities, and values, but did not experience the world in any sense. Aristotle was perfectly content with this. He argued that God couldn't care less about knowing the world, for the world was too mundane, too inferior. It wasn't worth knowing. Therefore, God simply contemplates his own thoughts in solitary splendor.

Whitehead became convinced that in order to render his metaphysics coherent, conceiving of God as one actual entity among other actual entities, God would also have physical prehensions. If so, he also directly experiences the world. Therefore, in this vision, God and the world form an ecosystem, wherein both contribute to each other. God provides each event with its aim or lure toward which it moves. The event actualizes itself, influenced by the possibilities that God has provided, but also becoming something in its self-production by appropriating elements out of its past. This result is then experienced by God. In this way, the world enriches God.[17]

In the classical view, God is what he is quite apart from whether the world exists or not. God's perfections are complete whether or not there is a world. If that is true, the world has no ultimate significance. For process theism, the world ultimately has its significance because of the way in which it enriches the divine experience. The classical view conceives of God as immutable and unchanging. It is based on the Greek idea that any change in a perfect being leads to corruption. Whitehead's argument, rather, is that the perfect is that which is capable of indefinite enrichment, capable of being enriched by that which is emerging.

We need also consider the matter of omniscience. In the classical view, God knows the future in detail. For him it is all mapped out. The problem always was to ascertain in what sense then we are free. We may be free in the sense that we are not compelled to act the way we do, but it remains an illusion to think that we could really act in an alternative way if God already knows the way we will act. There is only one way we can go. Whitehead argues that God does know everything there is to know, but he challenges the notion that the future can be known as if it were already actual. To know the future in the concrete detail which it will become is to know what is possible as if it were already actual. This is to know a contradiction. So God is always in process of experiencing what is new for him, namely, the course of the world as it fully actualizes its possibilities.

Even more drastically, process theism revises our understanding of divine power. Classically, God's power is seen in terms of omnipotence, and God is creator as the sole primary efficient cause of the world. In process theism God is primarily persuasive, creating more indirectly by providing the lure for each occasion whereby it can create itself.

It might seem, at first glance, that such modifications of God's knowledge and power are quite foreign to the biblical tradition. This may be, however, because we have grown accustomed to interpreting its message exclusively in classical categories. Process theism may provide a revised hermeneutic enabling us to understand and appropriate that message in a new and living way. As a philosopher, Whitehead was not overly concerned with this task, but for our purpose in providing an application of his thought to Christian theology, it is basic and central. Hence in the next two chapters we shall sketch some of the ways in which our understanding of the Bible can be enriched by the conceptuality of process theism, starting with selected themes from the Old Testament.

NOTES

1. *SMW*, p. 249.
2. *Alfred North Whitehead: Essays on His Philosophy,* ed. George L. Kline (Englewood Cliffs, N.J.: Prentice-Hall, 1963), p. 16.
3. See Victor Lowe, *Understanding Whitehead* (Baltimore: The Johns Hopkins University Press, 1962), p. 231.
4. Bertrand Russell, *Portraits from Memory* (New York: Simon and Schuster, 1956), p. 96.
5. *Dialogues of Alfred North Whitehead,* as recorded by Lucien Price (Boston: Little, Brown, 1954), p. 151.
6. Letter to Victor Lowe of September 26, 1959, as recorded in *Understanding Whitehead*, p. 232.
7. For the nature of the original Lowell Lectures (1925) and Whitehead's appended material on the character of time see my study, "Whitehead's First Metaphysical Synthesis," *International Philosophical Quarterly* 17/3, (September 1977), pp. 251–64.
8. Russell, *Portraits from Memory,* p. 93. Frederic R. Crownfield argues that Whitehead's revised rationalism, based upon his own reflections on Paul Sarpi's *History of the Council of Trent,* gradually led him out of his earlier agnosticism. "Whitehead: From Agnostic to Rationalist," *The Journal of Religion* 57/4 (October 1977), 376–85.

9. *SMW,* p. 275.
10. *Ibid.*, p. 274.
11. *Ibid.*, p. 275.
12. *Ibid.*
13. *Ibid.*, p. 269.
14. *Ibid.*, p. 270.
15. *Ibid.*, p. 266.
16. *PR*, p. 521.
17. *Ibid.*, p. 532.

CHAPTER 2

Divine Persuasion in the Old Testament

Whitehead personally seems to have felt little affinity with the Old Testament. Psalm 24, for example, might be "magnificent literature," but "this worship of glory arising from power" could only be based on "a barbaric conception of God."[1] By contrast Whitehead greatly admired Plato's conviction "that the divine element in the world is to be conceived as a persuasive agency and not as a coercive agency. This doctrine should be looked upon as one of the greatest intellectual discoveries in the history of religion."[2]

This differentiation between persuasive and coercive power moves somewhat beyond the Old Testament context which rarely addresses itself to this particular contrast. Nonetheless its dominant experience of divine power seems to emphasize coercive elements, with the symbols for power drawn heavily from the military and political spheres. Its roots are found in the very early tradition that Yahweh is a God of war:

> Sing to the Lord, for he has triumphed gloriously; the horse and his rider he has thrown into the sea. (Ex. 15:21)

> In the greatness of thy majesty thou overthrowest thy adversaries; thou sendest forth thy fury, it consumes them like stubble. (Ex. 15:7)

Throughout its history Israel relied upon the military prowess of Yahweh, first in the prosecution of holy war in defense of the tribal amphictyony, then against the enemies of the Lord's anointed (Psalm 2), and finally in expectation of the destruction of all powers oppressing Israel in the last day. "Does evil befall a city, unless the Lord has done it?" (Amos 3:6b). He has all power, both to create and to destroy, and that destructive power could also be turned against Israel itself. The entire prophetic corpus ends on that note of dire warning, "lest I come and smite the land with a curse" (Mal. 4:6).

Exclusive concern with divine power, however, distorts the texture of biblical experience, which does not systematically articulate a series of doctrines carefully correlated with one another, such that each may safely be considered on its own merits. Rather, Israel bore witness to that action of God directly impinging upon the situation at hand, letting the total cumulative context make the necessary adjustments and modifications. God is free to act as he wills (Ex. 33:19), so the experience of what God is now doing is neither determined by nor could it possibly repudiate what God has already done. But by his covenant with Israel all of God's actions could be accepted and understood as expressions of his age-long struggle and personal confrontation with his people and not as mere displays of raw, naked force. Divine power was interfused with moral purity, as witnessed, for example, in the experience of Isaiah the year King Uzziah died (Isaiah 6). Yet no matter how august, how holy, or how destructive God's power might be, it was always experienced as the expression of a divine will in personal interaction with his people.

That context, however, is no longer our context. The history of God's dealings with Israel can no longer serve as the all-embracing horizon for our understanding of God, which must now be correlated with a greatly expanded world history, a scientific understanding of nature and man, and a drastically altered social and ethical situation. It would appear that only a philosophical structure can provide a sufficiently inclusive context suitable to our needs. Therefore the hermeneutical task calls for the translation of Israel's experience into a contemporary systematic and conceptual framework, one that can do justice to its historical concerns. Much hermeneutical discussion today centers upon options within existential thought. Without question existential emphases upon risk, subjective appropriation, and decision must be affirmed, and the call to authentic openness may be appreciated as a protest against impersonal ethical norms. But as a total context existential philosophy is methodologically too restrictive. If faith can only be expressed in terms of human encounter, such that we are precluded from using any cosmological framework in expressing our understanding of God, then we have no way of appreciating God's activity and manifestation of concern toward the rest of the created order. We are in danger of succumbing to a global anthropocentricity in our existential preoccupation, precisely at a time when members of the scientific community are reckoning with the strong probability of intelligent life inhabiting other worlds within our universe.

It is no accident, however, that the present hermeneutical concern in biblical circles received its impetus from existential concerns. For the problem was not so much how to update a first-century world view, as how to express the biblical experience within *any* systematic, cosmological framework. Insofar as a cosmology was able to articulate the biblical sense of divine sovereign power, it seemed destined to minimize any creaturely contribution to creation and to transform providence into determinism. In the official formulation of Christian doctrine, Whitehead complains, "the deeper idolatry, of the fashioning of God in the image of the Egyptian, Persian, and Roman imperial rulers, was retained. The Church gave unto God the attributes which belong exclusively to Caesar."[3]

Process theism involves the persistent effort to conceive God's activity primarily in terms of persuasion. It firmly opposes those views which from its perspective imply certain kinds of coercion within divine power. Here it is necessary to be precise as to what we mean by coercion. Not every cause which is not persuasive is therefore coercive. Nor is every efficient cause coercive, and every final cause persuasive. Coercion is readily understood on the experiential level of social or physical behavior, but its proper metaphysical definition is difficult to ascertain.

Not every limitation is coercive. The laws of logic, metaphysics, and nature (causal uniformities) in one sense limit what is possible, but they also structure it. I am not coerced by demands of consistency, nor by the law of gravity, nor by my inability to fly. Even within the realm of possibility so structured by logic, metaphysics, and causal regularity there is the further limitation that my present possibilities conform to the particular causal conditions of my past. What I can now become must emerge out of the totality of those past conditions impinging upon me. These dictate the overwhelming improbability of my becoming the next astronaut, or the next president. These past conditions may sometimes be felt as coercive, but they are not coercive *as such*. They are also the enabling conditions where I am presently able to actualize myself, since I can only actualize myself as the outcome of the past.

We may define coercion generally as *any restriction upon the range of real possibility which would otherwise be available.* This definition cannot be made fully precise, for it is impossible for the same event to have other causal conditions or actualizable possibilities than it in fact has. If they were different, that would be a different event. The event can only be compared with contrary-to-fact conditions, and then only in terms of those properties we intuitively feel would "ordinarily" or "normally" apply. A judgment about coercion is thus always comparative and relative.

In general, there are two ways in which effective real possibility can be restricted. The first way concerns what is usually thought of as efficient causation, the way in which past causal conditions affect present decisions. The nature, variety, and complexity of these conditions may either expand or restrict the range of alternative possibility open to us. Any external alteration of these past causal conditions which restricts the range of possibility otherwise available acts as a *restraint,* and is thus coercive.

On its own terms, classical theism is hardly coercive. God's efficient causality is that which creates each being as it is, enabling it to exercise whatever freedom it is capable of. If, however, freedom is precisely that which cannot be derived from any external agency, including God, because it is the intrinsic self-creativity of each occasion, then divine efficient causality may be perceived to be coercive. Here we are comparing alternative metaphysical frameworks. If, in terms of process theism, God acts fundamentally through final causation, and the range of real possibility is correlated solely to finite past causal conditions, then the addition of some divine efficient causality may act as a restraint.

Suppose God's efficient causality acts as one causal condition among the others. Then there is an additional factor the occasion must conform to. This additional factor cannot be an enabling factor, since the totality of finite causal factors was sufficient in itself to allow the occasion to actualize itself. It can only be a restricting factor.

Suppose the divine efficient causality unifies all the other causal conditions. If it does no more than simply transmit the totality of past finite conditions, it would not itself be peculiarly coercive, but then it would be difficult to see how *God's* causality made any difference. If this divine efficient causality transcends the past conditions in some unlimited way, then the occasion would be completely determined by its past, and could not exercise its own self-creativity. Such absolute determination would be coercive.

This consequence is usually mitigated in classical theism by the supposition that when I act, it is also God acting through me. Finite and ultimate causation coincide. This identification is not possible in process theism, which sees self-decision and divine persuasion, along with the multiplicity of past causal conditions, as distinct but indispensable and complementary aspects of every act of freedom. Moreover, if efficient causation is identified with *past* causation, then if God exercises complete efficient causation, the past usurps all the space for present self-determination. Strictly speaking, if God is omnipotent, having *all* power, we can have none.

There is also a second form of coercion which primarily affects final causation. The range of real possibility relative to past causal conditions may remain constant, but the effective options within this range may be curtailed by *threat*. Such threats disturb the evaluation of future possibilities for their own sakes by attaching to these possibilities further consequences which are so undesirable as to eliminate them from serious consideration. While threats are generally most effective in restricting our options, promises of rewards may also work in this way. A possibility may no longer be judged on its own merits, but in terms of the reward it promises. In the absence of such coercive measures, however, the evaluation of real possibilities is genuinely persuasive, and influences purposively creaturely decision. The absence of complete causal determination is a necessary but not a sufficient condition for persuasion; there must also be the evaluation of alternative possibility. For process theism, this evaluation ultimately stems from God and constitutes the way he acts in the world by divine persuasion.

Both Plato and Aristotle proposed that God acts upon the world by persuasion, but this suggestion was not picked up by the early church. Christian theology would be vastly different if the church fathers had done so instead of adhering closely to the Greek ideal of perfection as immutability. As a result the biblical tradition has rarely been interpreted in terms of divine persuasion. Yet there are a good many biblical themes that the concept of divine persuasion can appropriate and illuminate, particularly themes which are a source of embarrassment to exponents of classical omnipotence. In the remainder of this chapter we shall isolate features that illustrate divine persuasion drawn from the areas of creation, providence, and biblical authority, reserving for the next chapter the difficult theme of the interaction of persuasive and coercive elements within the biblical image of God as king.

Quite apart from biblical precedents, the temptation to interpret God's role in creation in terms of efficient power is extremely great. If the entire created order is dependent for its existence upon his will, then it must be subject to his full control. Such control of the creative process entails efficient causality, for the divine initiative must be prior to the outcome, and the effect must conform to its cause. Since this divine efficient causality was essentially unlimited, it was preeminently conceived as calling forth being from nothing. Man, like his fellow creatures, was a created substance ultimately brought into being solely through divine power. Yet once in being, man is capable of exercising his own freedom to the extent that God is willing to relinquish some areas within his complete control.

This basic model of divine creative control through efficient causality, however, is seriously defective in confronting the problem of evil, for then God ought to reduce the amount of unnecessary evil to a minimum and to curtail that exercise of human freedom which he foresees will go astray. Insofar as God controls the world, he is responsible for evil: directly in terms of the natural order, and indirectly in the case of man.

Divine persuasion responds to the problem of evil radically, simply denying that God exercises full control over the world. Plato sought to express this by saying that God does the best job he can in trying to persuade a recalcitrant matter to receive the impress of the divine forms. But the early church rejected this solution on the grounds that it establishes a cosmic dualism between God and evil which undercuts human responsibility for sin and denies the biblical witness to the essential goodness of creation. Process theism therefore faces the double task of making creation without control credible and of overcoming these objections to Plato's doctrine.

The notion of divine persuasion entails a twofold expansion of our traditional understanding of freedom. It cannot be limited solely to man as an exceptional privilege to be enjoyed on divine sufferance, but some degree of freedom or spontaneity must be accorded to all of God's creatures, even the lowly atom. Secondly, it is not so much that a being is first created and then acts, as that its responsive activity in actualizing its own potentiality is part of the creative process itself. Divine persuasion maximizes creaturely freedom by respecting the creature's own integrity in the very act of guiding its development toward greater freedom. God is not the cosmic watchmaker, but the husbandman in the vineyard of the world, fostering and nurturing its continuous growth throughout the ages; he is the companion and friend who inspires us to achieve the very best that is within us.

God's dialogue with his creation is not limited to man, but is manifest in the entire evolutionary process. The world's general advance toward increased complexity does not emerge by chance, but calls for a transcendent directing power constantly introducing richer possibilities of order as the occasion arises. God proposes and the world disposes. The creature may or may not embody that divine urge toward greater complexity, but insofar as that ideal is actualized, an evolutionary advance has been achieved. This process is directed but not controlled, for the necessary self-activity of the creature requires spontaneity of response. This spontaneity may be extremely minimal for elementary particles but it increases with every gain in complexity. Spontaneity matures as freedom. On the level of human freedom it becomes possible for this divine urge to leave the biological sphere and be directed toward the achievement of civilization, and for the means of divine persuasion now to be consciously felt in terms of ethical and religious aspiration.[4] Not only we ourselves but the entire created order, whether consciously or unconsciously, is open to this divine persuasion, each in its own way.

Conceived in terms of persuasion, creation is the emergence of that which is genuinely new, requiring the new initiatives God is constantly introducing. It is not simply the recombination of the old, but depends upon novel structuring possibilities hitherto unrealized in the temporal world. The emergence of life is perhaps the single most dramatic example on this planet, yet even life also requires a material substratum of organic macromolecules out of which this radically novel form of existence could emerge. Creation is the fusion of novel form with inherited matter by the self-creative decision of the emergent creature. It cannot be simply conceived in terms of a creation out of nothing. In themselves the Old Testament traditions concerning creation, whether in the Priestly (Genesis 1) or Yahwistic (Genesis 2) accounts, or in Second Isaiah, Job, or the Psalms, do not insist upon this. Creation out of nothing is first mentioned in the Apocrypha: 2 Macc. 7:28.

Basically this doctrine was designed as a protective measure against Greek speculation designed to safeguard the essential goodness of God's creation and man's responsibility in the fall. It affirms that there is no recalcitrant evil external to man and the other creatures out of which the world must be made. Process theism can certainly agree with the intent behind this safeguard. God's creative persuasion is wholly good, and the symbol of the fall may be generalized to apply to the gap between divine purpose and creaturely actualization in every creature. This is the point of identity between creation and fall to which Tillich has alluded.[5] Evil enters the world through creaturely response, not from some preexistent chaos God is forced to work with.

Divine persuasion illuminates our understanding of the creative Word. Classically, the divine Word in John's prologue is the Logos, that basic structuring principle whereby the world is a cosmos and not a chaos. While true, this suggests a certain static character inconsistent with the emergent, improvisatory, evolutionary nature of our universe. God speaks in creation to each of his creatures, according to its particular situation, persuading it to bring forth the best that is within it; this speech is continuously being uttered anew. Here the consecutive acts, "And God said, let there be . . ." of the Priestly creation story, more adequately symbolize the dynamic character of the Word. Eight acts of divine speech schematically represent the untold multiplicity of divine urgings whereby God shaped this world, originally without form and void, into that which we may celebrate as a fit habitation for man.

The Word once spoken calls for a hearer, one capable of responding, whether on the human or subhuman level. If God says, "Let the earth put forth vegetation," we may understand the earth's bringing forth vegetation as its response to that divinely evoked aim (Gen. 1:11–12). As king of the universe, God's commands deserve such response. Speaking of the sun and the moon and the shining stars, the Psalmist writes: "For he commanded and they were created" (Ps. 148:5). It is not the case that he who commands our allegiance and obedience merely happens to be the creator of the world. It is the same Word spoken in creation that addresses us now, for the same purpose, which is the evocation of ever-increasing fulfillment of creaturely possibility. That Word spoken in the creation of the natural order also brought Israel into existence, and that Word incarnate in Jesus of Nazareth became the means whereby the church, the body of Christ, was created.

Israel itself was profoundly aware of the continuity of God's activity in the formation of the natural order and in the emergence of Israel. Psalms 135 and 136 directly juxtapose these two events in successive stanzas, while Second Isaiah fuses God's assault against the primeval waters of chaos with his assault against the waters of the Red Sea:

> Was it not thou that didst cut Rahab in pieces,
>   that didst pierce the dragon?
> Was it not thou that didst dry up the sea,
>   the waters of the great deep;
> that didst make the depths of the sea a way
>   for the redeemed to pass over? (Isa. 51:9b–10)

The collective memory of Israel concerning its own creation in the total Exodus event places the emphasis upon the intervening power of Yahweh, who "with a mighty hand and an outstretched arm, with great terror, with signs and wonders" (Deut. 26:8) brought them out of Egypt into a land flowing with milk and honey. At the same time, however, this memory preserves traditions concerning the utterance of a divine Word calling forth obedient response: the commission to Moses at the burning bush, and the commandments of Yahweh at Sinai. The covenant between Yahweh and Israel clearly symbolized the reciprocal character of effective creative activity: divine initiative and creaturely response. Israel's emergence and continued existence depended upon the conjoint presence of the divine Word and its own faithfulness to that Word, and this may serve as the paradigm for understanding creation.

From the standpoint of divine persuasion, providence is simply another way of looking at God's guidance of the historical process already manifest in creation. Classical omnipotence, however, in affirming God's sovereign control over the future, must look for a final break with the ambiguities of history in which God's goodness is unambiguously made manifest. Whatever the historical causes for the apocalyptic world view might be, its logical basis is a belief in God's full control of that which is to come. If God's activity is not readily apparent within the present vicissitudes of good and evil, that is because his hand is now stayed, but if God has the power to actualize the good unambiguously, then his goodness requires that he do so, and that right early. The more we feel the tension between God's sovereign omnipotence and the wickedness of the world, the greater will be our sense of expectation that the end must come quickly; any delay becomes increasingly intolerable. Moreover, since it is

God alone who can bring about this good, independently of the course of creaturely activity, it can be determined "from the foundations of the world" when and how this should be brought about.

Process theism cannot share this apocalyptic expectation because it sees the future as organically growing out of its past. All such actualization depends upon the vicissitudes of creaturely response. This does not preclude faith and hope, but such faith is a trusting and loyal devotion to God's purposes in the face of a risky and uncertain future, not belief in a divine timetable. Insofar as the whole creation trusts God to realize the purposes he proposes to us, then the good will triumph. The continued presence of evil, both in man and in the natural order, testifies to the very fragmentary realization of creaturely faith in God. Nonetheless, we may hope that the grace of God may be received and permeate all beings and in that hope do our part in the great task. Such hope prohibits other-worldly withdrawal, but calls upon us to redouble our efforts to achieve the good in the world.

Divine providence cannot be understood as the unfolding of a predetermined course of events. Prophecy is not prediction, but the proclamation of divine intent, dependent for its realization upon the continued presence of those conditions which called forth that intent and upon the emergence of the means whereby that intent may be realized. Isaiah's proclamation of the destruction of Judah was dependent upon the further, persistent opposition of Israel to God's commandments and upon the power of Assyria. For the prophets, then, God becomes the great improvisor and opportunist seeking at every turn to elicit his purpose from every situation: if not by the hand of Sennacherib, then by the hand of Nebuchadnezzar. If the nation of Israel will not actualize his redeeming purpose for man, then the task must be reserved for the faithful remnant. If that faithful remnant fails, we may then confess that God's aim becomes focused upon a single carpenter from Nazareth. This history is quite contingent and open-ended in its making, but it becomes the way in which God achieves his purposes in one way or another.

God's general, everlasting purpose is everywhere one and the same: the elicitation of the maximum richness of existence in every situation. Yet because creaturely response varies, the achievement of this good is highly uneven and follows many different routes. In biological evolution many other lines were tried—amphibians, reptiles, marsupials—before mammals emerged, and of the mammals only certain primates were responsive to the call to become human. Among men the response to God varied considerably, and even when that response was intense, God's address must be radically different depending upon their particular circumstances. The Word addressed to Abraham was not the same as the Word addressed to Ikhnaton or Gautama or Lao-Tzu.

Once that response has been made, it establishes a new situation permitting the intensification of divine purpose. Now God has increased potentialities with which to work. Abraham's journey establishes the nomadic conditions favorable to the emergence of a patriarchal cult whose God is no longer tied down to one particular locale. The cherished memory of a promised land then forms the background for the possibility contained within the call of Moses, while the traditions of the Exodus and Sinai in turn provide the framework in which the struggle between the prophets and the kings could occur. This enabled the prophets to declare their higher patriotism in proclaiming the destruction of their own land. It is the contingent character of this human response to the divine Word which generates the particularities that God then uses in the furtherance of his general aim at the intensification of value. The history of Israel assumes such religious importance because it proved to be the arena of a very dramatic intensification of divine purposes, generating both the expectation of the Lord's anointed and the awareness of God's involvement in the suffering of the world.

In addition to these themes of creation and providence, let us look briefly at the problem of biblical authority. As we all know, the God of the philosophers is not the same as the God of Abraham, Isaac, and Jacob. But why is this so? I think that classical theism found no really satisfactory answer to this question insofar as it maintained that all of God's attributes are strictly necessary. If God's control over the world is absolute in that it is independent of all creaturely contingencies, then God's activity may flow directly from his unchanging nature which was deemed wholly necessary and self-sufficient. But it is the business of philosophy to ascertain that which is purely necessary and universal, and any limitation placed upon philosophical reason ultimately appears to be arbitrary. If God's nature and activity are wholly necessary, then Hegel is right in supposing the biblical God to be an historically conditioned, concrete guise of that which finds its purest expression in the philosophical Absolute.

Classical theism has a penchant for universality, thus encroaching upon the proper dominion of philosophy, which has its own specific procedures and canons for evidence. Yet classical theism is acutely aware of its divergence from most philosophies. We are urged to believe various doctrines concerning the incarnation, the atonement, and the resurrection of Christ for which philosophical evidence or argument is quite inadequate, on the grounds that in these religious matters human knowledge can never suffice. Yet as Brand Blanshard has recently written:

> The world seemed to me one whole, and reason [meaning in this context our natural cognitive faculties] the only instrument we had with which to explore it. But if so, could the standards of belief that we applied in philosophy and science be dropped when we turned to religion? . . . There seemed to me to be an ethics of belief whose clear mandate was "Adjust your belief to the evidence," and I could not see why, if this was valid for common sense and science, it should not be valid for religion also.[6]

It is no accident that the leading exponents of process theism have shied away from revelatory or kerygmatic theology. Even Charles Hartshorne, whose "metaphysics of love" seeks to portray the salient features of Christian faith, establishes his conclusions solely upon philosophical and even rationalistic criteria. There is an unspoken skepticism of traditional beliefs which lack sufficient philosophical justification. Yet this need not be so. The logic of divine persuasion, moreover, requires us to recognize the limitation of the philosophical approach to God, not within its proper domain, to be sure, but with respect to the totality of divine activity. Process theism recognizes that God possesses both necessary and contingent features, while philosophy can only satisfactorily examine the necessary ones. Regarding these contingent features, we must resort to other methods, and here respect the evidence of historical testimony. Only because classical theism tended to conceive of all of God's attributes as universal and necessary, and thus properly within the scope of philosophical scrutiny, did such a problem ever arise.

God's generic attributes are necessary, and his steadfast purpose is everlasting, but his experience and activity are dependent upon the contingencies of the world. God's total experience of the world is constantly growing and being enriched by the world's growth. God's concrete response to the world in evoking the maximum value from every situation must be constantly shifting with new circumstances and can only be fully relevant to the world insofar as it is sensitive to these contingent developments. But if philosophical inquiry thus discovers contingent aspects in God's full actuality, it also discovers the intrinsic limits of its own inquiry into the mystery of God, for no amount of ingenious argument can deduce the concrete, historical character of that which happens to be, but which could have been otherwise.

Process is the abstract, necessary matrix whose contingent actualization is history. It is quite appropriate to speak of the history of God's activity if this is bound up with concrete response to creaturely activity, as both biblical traditions and process theism can affirm. The Old Testament is above all a theological document, although we often fail to appreciate this in supposing that all theology must express itself in systematic, universal concepts. Its medium of expression is historical recital, which concentrates not on what God necessarily is but on what he has contingently done.

Process philosophy can complement this biblical recital by providing a description of the necessary conditions whereby such contingent divine activity is possible, just as the biblical recital can complement this abstract philosophical outline by giving it specific, concrete historical contours. This historical development is completely open-ended, for process thought does not impose any particular pattern of historical development upon history, since God is ever resourceful in finding new perfections for creation to strive for. The perfections aimed at are concrete and particular, arising out of the historical contingencies: a promised land and a long-awaited Messiah for Israel. Process theism need not dissolve these particularities into symbolic manifestations of universal truth, since it can proclaim a God vitally interested in precisely these particularities whose activity is shaped by their peculiar character. These aims do not lose their particularity in being broadened to embrace all mankind, since from the divine perspective man is only one particular form of creation.

Our justification for the appeal of divine persuasion is broadly philosophical: its inherent reasonableness, its applicability to all we know about the world we live in, and its consonance with our best ethical and religious insights. As such, it is at least a partially alien criterion by which to appreciate biblical traditions, since their understanding of divine power is rather different, a subject we shall turn to in the next chapter. We can recommend process theism, however, for the hermeneutical task of translating these traditions into a systematic context appropriate to our contemporary situation, without thereby losing Israel's peculiar witness to the action of God in its history.

History need not be solely an immanent process which can at best point only symbolically to the divine, for that historical involvement may also shape the concrete actuality of God himself. Since it is in the particular, historical way that God was able to intensify his purposes through the agency of Israel that we experience our salvation, the Bible as the historical record of that way possesses authority for our lives. That authority cannot be found in its particular concepts of the divine nature, for these concepts must be open to correction and revision from whatever source is open to us. Yet in the absence of any comparable witness to the intensification of divine purpose for man this historical recital is indispensable. We may perhaps want to explain and understand Isaiah's experience somewhat differently, but that Isaiah did experience God's glory can only be discovered from the historical record. We can best proclaim God's saving acts for us by retelling Israel's history. If our retelling is selective, being told in systematic terms appropriate to our own age, we are only following the practice of the judges and the prophets themselves.[7]

NOTES

1. *RM,* p. 55.
2. *AI,* p. 213.
3. *PR,* p. 520.
4. See *RM,* p. 119.
5. Paul Tillich, *Systematic Theology,* vol. 2 (Chicago: The University of Chicago Press, 1957), pp. 39–44.
6. Brand Blanshard, "Rationalism in Ethics and Religion" in Peter A. Bertocci, ed., *Mid-Twentieth Century American Philosophy: Personal Statements* (New York: Humanities Press, 1974), p. 40.
7. Two such examples of this selective retelling of Israel's past may be found in Joshua 24 and Ezekiel 20.

CHAPTER 3

Divine Sovereignty

With respect to the question of divine power, as we saw in the last chapter, classical theism came to accept the model of efficient causation. This model can make good sense of many of the biblical traditions, but not of all: God's particular involvement in human history, his apparent lack of knowledge concerning the future in some of the earlier narratives, his suffering, his willingness on occasion to change his mind. These traditions could be comfortably suppressed as crude anthropomorphisms as long as confidence in the model of divine efficient causation remained strong, but that model has become vulnerable in recent centuries because it cannot do justice to the problem of evil or account adequately for creative freedom. An alternative, now emerging in theism, is the model of divine persuasion.

Given these two philosophical perspectives, the coercive and the persuasive, the biblical witness to divine power seems inconsistent. Each can explain what the other cannot. Between them they can account for all the texts, broadly speaking, but they seem mutually incompatible. From another perspective, however, this mixture of persuasive and coercive elements becomes readily intelligible. One of the basic biblical images, particularly with respect to the symbolization of divine power, is the figure of the king. A king does not rule by being the efficient cause or maker of anything. His rule is largely persuasive; it is effective insofar as his subjects are obedient to the royal commands. That rule, however, is not *purely* persuasive, for the king has access to coercive measures to apply to those who refuse to comply.

In a discussion of power and obedience in the primeval history, George W. Coats has recently outlined the logic of this position.[1] He emphasizes the element of persuasion involved in the divine commands given to the man and the woman in the garden. This element of persuasion respects their freedom and integrity. "So, as long as the human creature can be persuaded to obey the limitations placed on him by his creator, creation will be in its proper order. Yet, what happens when the human creature remains unpersuaded?"[2] "God kicked man out of the garden to his death, away from the tree of life. And he made it impossible for man to get back in. There is no divine persuasion here. There is only divine coercion, a divine sentence of death for the disobedient creature."[3] Later on, he concludes:

> Thus, the God who persuades and the God who judges the unpersuaded stand in tension. This tension is an integral part of creation theology. Moreover, the grandiose, prideful, vain, and egotistical man lives in tension with the call to obedience and its corresponding limitations on power. If he goes too far in obedience, he may lose his freedom, his maturity, his necessary grandiosity. If he goes too far in his freedom, he loses his source of power, indeed, his life. The mature son celebrates those tensions before God as a responsible king who rules God's creation. And in the celebration he receives both his life and his power.[4]

Persuasion and coercion stand in tension, but the same God can apply both if he is primarily conceived of as a king exercising his royal authority. In the Priestly creation story, persuasion was sufficient. The cosmic ruler commanded, and the world faithfully executed those commands. Because of this faithful obedience, the created order could meet with God's full approval: "behold, it was very good" (Gen. 1:31). But as Coats points out, problems arise with disobedience, particularly when man oversteps the limits of his power. God may be patient and long-suffering, but sooner or later he must intervene to vindicate his rule. As king God is judge, the one charged with maintaining justice by overthrowing the oppressor and rescuing the oppressed.

There is no question but that this image of God as king poses serious difficulties for process theism, for it not only highlights elements of divine coercion but offers a coherent account of their presence. In moving back from philosophical to biblical concepts, however, we find ourselves in a domain of shifting and fluid patterns, and the image of God as king is no exception. Generally speaking, this poses no problem as long as both the persuasive and the coercive elements are balanced against one another, and the only issue concerns the relative importance of each. But the inner dynamic of Israel's experience of God's sovereignty over history leads inexorably to the view that he exercises absolute control over the future. In that moment there is no longer any divine persuasion remaining, nor logically any creaturely freedom. At this juncture, however, just when it appears that there is no room at all for any affirmation of divine persuasion, Jesus' proclamation of the kingdom of God introduces a radically new way of experienceing God's sovereignty as the power of the future. As the power of the future, God's activity is not only purely persuasive but does not need coercive measures to achieve its purposes. Thus while process theism can only do partial justice to many of the images of divine kingship in the Bible, and none to some, it may be the model most appropriate to the final image emerging from this tradition.

The shift from a prophecy to apocalypticism gave an important stimulus toward views of divine determinism. As long as God is conceived as operating by persuasion, he must effect his purposes indirectly, through the agency of historical forces. For persuasion depends upon obedience, whether that obedience is freely given, or unwittingly exacted as in the case of Nebuchadnezzar and Cyrus. For this reason divine persuasion must work with existing historical realities to shape them toward desired ends. Once, however, God is conceived as exerting his power directly, or by means of heavenly creatures wholly subservient to his will, the actual deployment of historical forces becomes irrelevant to the realization of divine purposes. Thus the imagination of the apocalyptic seer is freed from the constraints imposed upon the prophet. He is freed to dream of God's decisive, unambiguous act to eradicate all evil, as the ambiguities of divine action in the historical process recede into the background. History becomes simply an interval of waiting, negatively contrasted to this coming, glorious day. But it is fully known and measured, else why should it endure so long? Since God is fully in control, he should vindicate himself right early. The apocalypticist's task is only to explain the delay and indicate signs of its coming.[5]

The seeds of this transition from prophecy to apocalyptic may be found in part in the trial speeches in Second Isaiah.[6] In these scenes the gods of the nations are brought before the ultimate judge, the Lord of Israel:

> Set forth your case, says the Lord;
>   bring your proofs, says the King of Jacob.

Let them bring them, and tell us what is to happen.
Tell us the former things, what they are,
    that we may consider them,
that we may know their outcome;
    or declare to us the things to come.
Tell us what is to come hereafter,
    that we may know that you are gods;
do good, or do harm,
    that we may be dismayed and terrified.
Behold, you are nothing, and your work is nought;
    an abomination is he who chooses you. (Isa. 41:21–24)

At stake here is the reliability of divine promise and threat. The Lord declared to Israel "the things to come" in his threats to destroy Israel and Judah for their sins, and he made good on those threats. Now he is about to fulfill his promises and bring the captives back to Jerusalem. The Lord has the power to bring about the aims he envisages; he accomplishes his purpose. These other gods may declare what they are going to do through their prophets, but nothing ever happens. They don't come through on their promises.

So interpreted, Second Isaiah's message remains wholly within the prophetic framework. We can rest content in the reliability of God's promise, while also looking about to discover what will be the instrumentality for achieving this purpose. God can bring about his goals by one means or another as he seeks to exercise his persuasive powers.

But the passage can also be interpreted another way. The gods of the nations cannot declare the future because they do not know it, and it is this lack of knowledge which proves that they are not gods. Moreover, God knows the future because he has the power to control it, and the future must conform to that control. God's declaration of what is to come is then a prediction based on certain knowledge, not a promise he intends to fulfill. Omnipotence here becomes the foundation for omniscience, and the groundwork has been set for a thoroughgoing determinism. This never occurs in apocalypticism, however, for in that vision God only controls the major events of history. He does not interfere with the freedom of those addressed, who are urgently summoned to repentance and obedience.

The very human yearning for vindication in the midst of ambiguous circumstances thus generates an inexorable pressure upon the logic of divine sovereignty. We seek to be sure of God's actions, and not to rest content with his promises. This pressure undermines the unstable balance that existed between persuasion and coercion, leading ultimately to the elimination of human freedom, at least theoretically, in the face of a completely determined future. And yet, paradoxically, the apocalyptic contains within itself the seeds of human freedom, which achieved their decisive breakthrough in the proclamation of Jesus. For the apocalyptic transposed the decisive locus of divine sovereignty from the present to the future. As we shall see, this understanding of God as future, or more precisely, as the power of the future effective in the present, permits a renewed appropriation of divine persuasion and human freedom.[7]

Apocalyptic Judaism acknowleged God's lasting, ever-present sovereignty in his lordship over Israel, but in a rather perfunctory way. This sovereignty at best was a limited and hidden one, for Israel was in slavery to the Gentile nations who reject the reign of God. God's reign and the reign of the Gentiles over Israel form an intolerable contradiction. So all hope and concern was directed toward God's future reign, when Israel would be freed, and the whole world would see and acknowledge God as king.

Jesus shared this focus of concern toward God's coming, future reign. Jeremias reports as an assured result: "Nowhere in the message of Jesus does the *basileia* (kingdom) denote the lasting reign of God over Israel in this age."[8] But unlike Jewish apocalypticists before him, and Christian apocalypticists after him, he refused to speculate concerning the signs of the end that must be fulfilled. He does not seek to explain why God's kingdom has been delayed so long, for he was grasped by its immediacy. With John the Baptist (cf. Matt. 3:2), Jesus proclaimed that "the kingdom of God is at hand" (Mark 1:15 par.) "God is coming, he is standing at the door, indeed, he is already there."[9] He promises his disciples that some of them will "see the kingdom of God come with power" in their lifetimes (Mark 9:1). The incident concerning the barren fig tree (Mark 11:12–14) may portray this expectation of an imminent end even more vividly, if Jeremias is correct in suspecting an Aramaic imperfect with an originally future significance behind the Greek text. Then Jesus, in finding the tree merely in leaf, uttered not a curse but a prediction: "No one will eat fruit from you again" because the end-times will be upon us even before those figs become ripe.[10]

The consummation of the kingdom is a purely divine act. Only the Father knows and decides when that will be. When it comes, it will come suddenly. We can do nothing to hasten its day, nor avert its coming. Jesus scorns those who would try to bring the kingdom about through their own efforts: "From the days of John the Baptist until now the kingdom of heaven has suffered violence, and men of violence take it by force" (Matt. 11:12). Nonetheless, the very imminence of this coming great event exerts tremendous power over the present moment, endowing it with extreme urgency. Elisha was allowed to say farewell to his family (1 Kings 19:20), but Jesus does not grant his disciples this permission (Luke 9:61–62). Nor can he permit a son to fulfill the elemental duty of mourning his father the customary six days: "Leave the dead to bury their own dead" (Luke 9:60). Those who fail to heed the call, who are not galvanized into action by the presence of this irrupting kingdom, are simply dead, perpetuating the existence of this old age. Every hour is precious, too precious to be taken up with mourning. The dead must be called into the world of life before it is too late.[11] When the crunch is on, we must act quickly, and decisively, taking extraordinary measures. Even conniving old stewards about to be thrown out of work know this (Luke 16:1–7). Jesus' instructions when he sent forth the disciples to preach the kingdom also express this urgency to lose no time. "Salute no one on the road" (Luke 10:4): do not tarry in exchanging greetings, or join caravans traveling the same direction. This command was more offensive then than now, because of the deeper significance of salutations then in communicating the peace of God.[12] Likewise each town was given its chance, but if its inhabitants do not respond, move on quickly. "When they persecute you in one town, flee to the next; for truly, I say to you, you will not have gone through all the towns of Israel, before the Son of man comes" (Matt. 10:23).

Something momentous did happen shortly with the resurrection of the living Christ as the dynamic, coordinating agency energizing a radically new communal reality,[13] but this was not the expected consummation of the kingdom. Insofar as Jesus' expectations are to be understood out of the traditional apocalyptic which he undoubtedly shared, they went unfulfilled. But Jesus also spoke of the present immediacy of this future kingdom, for this future reality exerted its power upon present actions. The kingdom of God in Jesus' preaching cannot be interpreted as either simply future or simply present; recent New Testament scholarship has abundantly shown this. It is in this peculiar tension between the future and the present that Jesus introduces a novel element ultimately destructive of the apocalyptic framework within which most of the New Testament is articulated.

Jesus proclaimed: "The kingdom of God has come near,"[14] which means more than simply that it was expected to arrive at some not too distant date in the future. Its nearness is also a qualitative measure of its power in affecting the present, a power which has already come to be felt. This future reality exerts its own power, more or less felt in varying degrees of nearness or distance. As this nearness was experienced in all of its power and poignancy, it was natural to assume, given the apocalyptic expectations of the day, that the long awaited kingdom of God was also chronologically near as well. But the experienced nearness of the kingdom may be independent of its chronological date, since it applies directly only to the *power* which the future exerts in the present.

This proclamation is also coupled with a summons to repentance and faith. The power of this nearness does not affect us indifferently, shunting us to and fro in the manner of a physical force acting in terms of efficient causation. This power addresses our freedom, eliciting a response of acceptance or hostility. Its power lies precisely in its capacity to call forth our freedom, for it stirs us to our very depths. The possibilities of repentance and faith require the fullest exercise of freedom, as they involve the transformation of our own selfhood.

For the purpose of a fuller analysis, we introduce a threefold distinction between the power of the past, the power of the present, and the power of the future. These three powers interpenetrate; they require each other, as all contribute to the actualization of each action or event. These are the ways process philosophy sees the three modes of time to be ingredients in causation. Whitehead conceives of the actuality as producing itself out of the way in which it appropriates its antecedent causes. The locus of productive activity thereby shifts from the past causes to the present event, which is active in virtue of its own power. The past causes determine the content of the present actuality, but only as this content is appropriated and unified by the present activity. Causation is here understood on analogy with perception: nothing is perceived unless we actively engage our attention in perceiving, yet what we perceive is dependent upon content derived from our environment. The power of the present selects and unifies this past content, so that the past is effective in the present only insofar as it is taken up into the present by the power of the present. Not all past actuality can be appropriated by the present because it contains conflicting and incompatible tendencies. Our freedom lies in the power of the present to select and to organize that which we inherit from the past.

In the absence of direction, however, such freedom would merely effectuate random combinations of the past. Freedom is responsibly exercised in the light of future possibilities, which become lures insofar as they are valued. Thus we may describe free actualization as the bringing of the past into the present by the power of the present responding to the lure of the future. The future is just as causally effective as the past, though each in its own way. This would be denied on the ordinary assumption that causes produce their effects, for all productive agency must be vested in actualities, and there can be no future actualities. But in Whitehead's reversal of our ordinary assumption, productive agency is vested in the actuality presently coming into being, so that its causes are merely passive objects to be appropriated. Future possibilities are just as objective as such past actualities, and hence are equally capable of exerting causal power to the extent that they are taken up into the present. The particular valued possibilities which shape our actions come from many sources, but ultimately, Whitehead argues, they derive from the creative activity of God. God is the ultimate power of the future, rescuing the world from degeneration into chaos by the relentless provision of ever-new creative possibilities for the world to actualize.

The interacting roles of these three powers may be seen in Paul's contrast between flesh and spirit (Gal. 5:16–24). The flesh cannot simply mean the body, since the works of the flesh include idolatry, enmity, jealousy, and the like—passions not obviously rooted in our biological makeup. Yet the word "flesh" indicating our biological heritage is enormously suggestive. It embraces all of our habits and "natural" desires, and constitutes the power of the past as effective in our lives. Spirit, in contrast, testifies to the power of the future. Flesh and spirit are forever in tension with one another, for in every decision we determine whether our future goals will shape our past inclinations, or vice versa, and to what extent. They require each other, for without the past, there is nothing which can come into being in the present, while without the future, there is nothing for the present to become. Their constant struggle, moreover, indicates that these two powers alone do not determine what is. There must also be the power of the present, which is our inmost being, by which we respond to the future by means of the past, and to the past by means of the future.

The power of the future does not reside in some future actuality. This is a contradiction in terms if, in our freedom, we face a genuinely open future, such that nothing is actual until it has been actualized in the present. Moreover, it is not as if this awaited actuality first exerts power when it becomes actual in the present. For any power it exerted then would be the power of the past or the present, not the power of the future. To understand the power of God, then, we must focus our attention on how the future can be effective in the present. It is precisely on this point that Jesus' teaching is liberating, for it portrays this future kingdom as it impinges upon the present. Both dimensions are crucial. If the kingdom is simply a present reality, then it is just one more actuality among others in our present world, mysteriously hidden from view. If the kingdom is simply future, then it exerts no power to which the present must respond, but remains merely an inert possibility we hope someday might be realized. It is the energizing of possibilities by divine appetition that constitutes the power of the future in the present, the nearness of God's reign.

In the controversy concerning Beelzebul, Jesus declared: "But if it is by the finger of God that I cast out demons, then the kingdom of God has come upon you" (Luke 11:20; cf. Matt. 12:28). This manifestation of divine power signifies the nearness of the kingdom, which in the apocalyptic expectation Jesus shared might be imagined to be casting its shadows before it, if not already breaking into their midst. Apart from the association of experienced nearness with chronological nearness, however, this saying takes on almost the character of an analytic truth: the exercise of God's power is the way in which he reigns among us. The kingdom of God is not a political commonwealth but signifies rather God's active ruling, which must be present where the divine power is manifest. By using the term "kingdom of God," with its indelible future orientation, however, Jesus implies that God's power *is* this power of the future, for it is this future reigning of God which is actualized in the present by means of this ministry of exorcism.

If this future reigning is already effective in our world, then we may anticipate the conditions of the age to come here and now. The experienced nearness of God's reigning power justifies Jesus' anticipatory actions: his table-fellowship with the lost sheep of Israel looking forward to the messianic banquet; the gift of God's forgiveness, reserved for messianic times (Mark 2:5); his preaching of a new, eschatological Torah designed for this new coming age. This was a time for new wine, for new garments, bursting through the limits of the old (Mark 2:21–22). While this power is near, this is not a time for fasting, but for the feasting of the wedding (Mark 2:19).

The apocalyptic hope powerfully expresses our very human longing for an unambiguous display of God's activity. Israel characteristically looked for a future Day of the Lord, but Isaiah may have had the discernment to recognize that a Day of the Lord may have occurred in the events surrounding Sennacherib's attempted invasion of Judah in 701 B.C.[15] But it is difficult to discern the decisive action of God in the vicissitudes of this life. If our analysis of God's reigning as the power of the future is correct, it is not hard to see why this is so. The power of the future is effective only insofar as it is responded to by the power of the present, and that response is usually highly fragmentary, since it is also colored by the power of the past. None of these three powers actualizes anything independently of the others. This means that God as the power of the future is necessarily effective in all things, but it also means that nowhere is he the sole agent. If so, the straightforward apocalyptic hope is an idle dream, resting upon a misconception of how God acts.

There is also another difficulty. If the kingdom of God were to become a present reality, it would no longer be future. Thus the reigning of God is forever future, never capable of surrendering its futurity to present realization. This emphatically does not mean that the kingdom is infinitely distant and therefore unrealizable. It means rather that it is precisely as future that God's reign exerts its power, affording the opportunity for its realization here and now, however fragmentarily. We can confess, however, that God's sovereign majesty did draw nigh unto man in the person of Jesus Christ. Through Jesus' faithful response to the Father, his human activity became the vehicle for divine activity, for Jesus' own power of the present allowed the divine power of the future to be fully effective.

It is our contention, then, that Jesus' response to the present power of the coming kingdom implicitly undermined the apocalyptic expectation for an unambiguous display of divine majesty in this world, although he continued to share that hope. If so, what then happens to the consummation of the kingdom and the last judgment? Are these simply mythological accompaniments of this now unfounded apocalyptic hope?

The final judgment, which Jesus conceived as preparatory to the consummation,[16] cannot be lightly dismissed in our time. The possibility of major human catastrophe, whether by nuclear holocaust or by irreversible ecological disaster, is all too real. Seen in a wider perspective, the threat of destruction has always been present in a world containing a vast multiplicity of free centers of power potentially in conflict with one another. These are all held together in loose harmony by the pervasive influence of God as their coordinating agency. "If he should take back his spirit to himself, . . . all flesh would perish together, and man would return to dust" (Job 34:14–15). The entropic forces toward increasing disorder would take over to reduce this cosmos into chaos. If this coordinating activity is God's universal function, then it is by God's power that our own catastrophe has been averted this long. Jesus understood that God could both *shorten* (Mark 13:20) and *lengthen* the present time, as the parable of the barren tree indicates (Luke 13:6–9). "All human existence, hourly threatened by the catastrophe, lives in the interval of grace: 'Let it alone this year also, in case it perhaps bears fruit' (Luke 13:8f)."[17]

Catastrophe as such is the result of destructive causal forces existent in the world; its power derives from past actuality as it impinges upon us, and not directly from God. Nevertheless, these destructive forces may on occasion be acting in response to divine directives.[18] They express the wrath of God, insofar as God judges existing orders and structures as worthy of destruction.[19] Existing structures may be obstructing the realization of new relevant values, and to that extent be evil, deserving to be destroyed. The revolutionary fervor of the oppressed may be inspired by a holy zeal. But the judgment of destruction is always ambiguous; many values only possible in terms of the old order will never be realized, even though the destruction of that order permits other kinds of value to emerge. The destruction is experienced as disaster by those who cling to the values of the old order, but is welcomed as liberation and opportunity by those seeking the new order. Because God's judgment is always for the sake of some further ideal, it can never be final in any absolute sense. His is always the power of the future, and therefore cannot motivate any absolute termination beyond which there is no future. Nevertheless, divine judgment may be final with respect to this present age and the ideals it seeks to exemplify.

God's judgment takes place through the instrumentalities of this world, but the consummation of the kingdom we long for must be an unambiguously divine event. For that very reason it cannot be a future event, as every event in this temporal world requires the conjoint activity of both God and creatures. Our irreducible freedom, moreover, means that we finally determine, through our own present power, how effective God's future power will be. This is a paradoxical and intolerable result from the standpoint which assumes that all power is measured in terms of the capacity to produce results, and God's supreme power is manifest in his productive creation of this world *ex nihilo*. Denying God the power to replace this world by another would be tantamount to reducing him to impotence and inactivity. On the other hand, if productive activity is vested in becoming, in our present power to produce ourselves, then God's supreme activity lies in his creation of himself, not the world. Rather than seek the consummation in some future event in which God affects the world, we should find it in the continuing way in which the world affects God.

Apart from the world God has neither past nor future, but is pure presence. Nontemporal, he creates himself as the envisagement of the infinitude of all pure possibilities.[20] Just as the world acquires a future from God, so God acquires a past from the world. Each individual creature receives its past from the other creatures of the world, and its future ultimately from God, and out of these creates a new present. God's presence is internal to himself, derived from his nontemporality, but out of that and the past which he receives from the world he creates a new future, as he transforms his pure possibilities into real possibilities, that is, realizable possibilities under the conditions of the world. Thus we do not say that God is a future reality which does not yet exist. Most properly, he is a nontemporal actuality who influences us by the future he now creates; by means of the real possibilities he persuades the world to actualize.

To be sure, the existence of nontemporal actuality is different from that of temporal actuality, for temporal actualities influence us as past efficient causes. That does not make him any less existent, but it does mean that his presence is felt through an entirely different mode, the future.

Moreover, this creation of the future provides God with a way of achieving the final consummation. For it is by means of the conceptual richness of his inexhaustible pure possibilities that God is able to absorb into himself the multifariousness of the world, overcoming the evil of its destructive conflicts through the higher harmonies this infinite imagination provides. God experiences

> every actuality for what it can be in such a perfected system—its sufferings, its sorrows, its failures, its triumphs, its immediacies of joy—woven by rightness of feeling into the harmony of the universal feeling . . . . The revolts of destructive evil, purely self-regarding, are dismissed into their triviality of merely individual facts; and yet the good they did achieve in individual joy, in individual sorrow, in the introduction of needed contrast, is yet saved by its relation to the completed whole. The image—and it is but an image—the image under which this operative growth of God's nature is best conceived, is that of a tender care that nothing be lost.[21]

This weaving together of the actual and the ideal is the consummation of the world in God's experience,[22] but it is also our future, since the ideals used to bring the actuality experienced by God into harmonious unity thereby also become ideals and lures for actualization in the temporal world. "For the perfected actuality passes back into the temporal world, and qualifies this world so that each temporal actuality includes it as an immediate fact of relevant experience. For the kingdom of heaven is with us today . . . . It is the particular providence for particular occasions."[23] The kingdom of heaven, as Whitehead understands it, is the perfected actuality of God as incorporating within himself the ongoing process of the world. It also provides the power of the future as operative in the present as the source of those aims we seek to realize in faith.

This sense of the kingdom of God is eloquently evoked in another passage from Whitehead's writings. Its explicit topic is religion *per se*, but perhaps it describes more accurately the epitomization of religion that we find in Jesus' proclamation of the kingdom:

> Religion is the vision of something which stands beyond, behind, and within, the passing flux of immediate things; something which is real, and yet waiting to be realized; something which is a remote possibility, and yet the greatest of present facts; something that gives meaning to all that passes, and yet eludes apprehension; something whose possession is the final good, and yet is beyond all reach; something which is the ultimate ideal, and the hopeless quest.[24]

Jesus' proclamation of the coming kingdom of God was open-ended, although clothed in the specific apocalyptic imagery of the day. In this particular form the kingdom has not come with power, at least not as soon as the early Christians eagerly awaited it. Yet the sovereignty of God was effectively manifest in those days. This Jesus, who was killed, God raised up and made both Lord and Christ (Acts 2:32, 36). The resurrection of Jesus whereby he became the dynamic directing agency of a new corporate reality, the body of Christ, exhibits the creative power of God for man in a way never before achieved. This was a new biological emergence, a vital breakthrough in the evolutionary history of the world, made possible by the creative order made available by God in that specific situation. In the resurrection Jesus became the Christ as the incarnation or actualization of the divine Word addressed to the human situation, thereby realizing the kingdom or sovereignty of God in our midst.

This is our theme in chapter five. It is also our Christology, specified in terms of the resurrection. We understand by the Christ the realization of that specific aim or future possibility appropriate to our human condition, an aim which Christians confess was fully actualized in Jesus of Nazareth. Since this christological proposal emphasizes the contingent specificity of the divine aim in Christ, it is not an aim given to everyman, nor is it an aim which primarily reveals to us the character of God rather than his specific address to man. On these counts it considerably diverges from other proposals in process Christology. Thus we shall preface our examination of the resurrection by a consideration of several other Christologies formulated in a process vein, indicating the strengths and difficulties of each. In this way we shall see more clearly the criteria proposed for an adequate process Christology, and be in a position to judge how well they apply to an interpretation of the resurrection, the central event in the life of the church, both then and now.

Our proposal also entails a distinction between the Christ, that Word or creative possibility specifically addressed to the human situation and actualizable by a man, and the Logos, which is the totality of creative possibilities inherent in the primordial or nontemporal nature of God, actualizable by the diverse creatures appropriate to them, including intelligent living beings on other worlds. In limiting their concerns to man, the church fathers made all too quickly an identification between the Christ and the second member of the Trinity. It is difficult to persuade ourselves of the untenability of this identification without a full exploration of the problem of extraterrestrial life, so we shall undertake this as well in the next chapter in preparation for our christological proposal. In this way, too, we shall see the close correlation that exists between creation and salvation.

NOTES

1. George W. Coats, "The God of Death," *Interpretation* 29/3 (July 1975), 227–39.

2. *Ibid.,* pp. 230–31.

3. *Ibid.,* p. 231.

4. *Ibid.,* p. 238. For a vigorous defense of the claim that a process model of divine power includes both coercive and persuasive elements, see J. Gerald Janzen, "Modes of Power and the Divine Relativity," *Encounter* 36/4 (Autumn 1975), 379–406. Janzen's essay originated as a response to an earlier version of this chapter. Its exegetical insights, particularly concerning Job and Romans 8, are daring and challenging. Although we differ on at least one point in the interpretation of Whitehead's philosophy (he holds the system to require that God acts efficiently by mediating to present events finite efficient causes derived from the past), I do not see how his God acts coercively in any of the senses outlined in the previous chapter. To act coercively God would have to restrict the range of real possibility otherwise available to a given event. Since past events already restrict this range, it is not further restricted by having these events mediated to the present event through God. Other than mediating the past, his God seems to act in a purely persuasive manner.

5. The apocalypticist typically believes that God must come quickly because he cannot any longer tolerate the evil of the world. As we shall see, this was not Jesus' reason for proclaiming the nearness of the kingdom.

6. See Isa. 41:1–5, 21–29; 43:8–15; 44:6–8, 21–22; 45:20–25.

7. The phrase, "the power of the future effective in the present," is borrowed from the writings of Wolfhart Pannenberg, though perhaps I use it in a different sense than he intends. As Pannenberg correctly notes, Whitehead himself gives no constitutive role to the future in his philosophy: see *John Cobb's Theology in Process,* ed. David Ray Griffin and Thomas J. J. Altizer (Philadelphia: Westminster Press, 1977), p. 136. Pannenberg convinces me that he should, and I believe such an extension of Whitehead's philosophy is not inconsistent with its basic principles. See my proposal, "A Whiteheadian Basis for Pannenberg's Theology," *Encounter* 38/4 (Autumn 1977), 307–17, and my conversation with Pannenberg, "A Dialogue about Process Philosophy," *ibid.,* pp. 318–24.

8. Joachim Jeremias, *New Testament Theology: The Proclamation of Jesus* (New York: Scribner's, 1971), pp. 101–2.

9. *Ibid.,* p. 102.

10. *Ibid.,* p. 132.

11. *Ibid.*

12. *Ibid.,* p. 133.

13. See Chapter 5.

14. Luke 10:11; cf. Luke 10:9; Mark 1:15; Matt. 3:2; 4:17; 10:7.

15. See Isa. 22:1–14, interpreting the perfect tense as past rather than as "prophetic future." See also A. Joseph Everson, "The Days of Yahweh," *Journal of Biblical Literature* 93 (1974), 329–37.

16. See Jeremias, *New Testament Theology*, pp. 122–41.

17. *Ibid.*, p. 140.

18. God's activity may be understood as indirectly coercive, but it is directly persuasive, becoming coercive only insofar as his aims are actualized in creaturely response. Here we diverge somewhat, perhaps, from Daniel Day Williams, who writes: "Certainly it is true that God does exercise coercive power. We cannot escape the fact when we look at the way in which the structures of life coerce us, smash our plans, seize us in the grip of their inevitabilities. God is not identical with those structures but His wrath is in them as they are related to the ultimate structures of value which is His own being" ("Time, Progress, and the Kingdom of God," in *Process Philosophy and Christian Thought*, ed. Delwin Brown, Ralph E. James, Jr., and Gene Reeves [Indianapolis: Bobbs-Merrill, 1971]; p. 461.

Williams's qualification, that God is not identical with those structures, indicates that the coercion itself ultimately comes from that which is not God, though perhaps mediated by him. It is true, however, that these structures themselves may in turn be derived from the actualization (at least in part) of values provided by God.

19. "Wrath" here is most appropriate, for as our minds feel and transmit the anger (and other passions) of our bodily feelings, so God internalizes those destructive intentions which conform with his solemn sense of justice. Otherwise his judgments would be cold and unfeeling, not drawing upon a rich undercurrent of passion ultimately derived from the world itself. On this point, see my essay on "Our Prayers as God's Passions," pp. 429–38 in *Religious Experience and Process Theology*, ed. Harry James Cargas and Bernard Lee (New York: Paulist Press, 1976). Yet as J. Gerald Janzen has masterfully shown in a careful exegesis of God's speech in Hos. 11:8, which he translates as "My heart transforms itself upon me/My change of mind grows fervent," God's love can overwhelm and transform such wrath, although preserving and including it within a greater integration: "Metaphor and Reality in Hosea 11," *Society of Biblical Literature 1976 Seminar Papers*, ed. George MacRae (Missoula: Scholars Press, 1976), pp. 413–45.

20. See chapter 7 outlining a process trinitarianism, note 5. The nontemporal act whereby the Father begets the Son "before all worlds" can also be conceived as the act whereby God creates himself.

21. *PR*, p. 525.

22. I have explored this theme more fully in "Divine Persuasion and the Triumph of Good," pp. 287–304 in *Process Philosophy and Christian Thought*, especially in the final section.

23. *PR*, p. 532.

24. *SMW*, pp. 267–68.

CHAPTER 4

Recent Process Christology

The philosophies of Whitehead and Hartshorne are undoubtedly deeply theistic in intention, but Christians looking them over for possible theological appropriation have often complained that they lack any Christology. Neither has developed any explicit theory concerning the nature of Christ, nor have any of their earlier followers, with one exception. This historical result used to be frequently regarded as evidence suggesting that no real Christology could be developed on process principles. This objection seems to stand refuted, *prima facie* at least, by the spate of essays during the past few years proposing a variety of process Christologies. We propose to examine some of these proposals to see what they achieve. Are they efforts to show how various christological assertions, derived elsewhere, can be rendered consistent with process categories, or are they genuinely dependent upon, and emergent from, the more distinctive features of process thought? In what ways can they be reconciled with one another? In summarizing the positive results of this survey we hope to prepare the way for the distinctive thrust of our own christological proposal that the body of Christ with the risen Lord as its head constitutes the next evolutionary emergence beyond man.

Before looking at these recent proposals, it will be instructive to take a glance at that one early exception, Lionel Thornton's *The Incarnate Lord*. The failure of this ambitious attempt to fuse an evolutionary concept of nature with a high Christology and an orthodox Trinitarianism has won few adherents among either students of Christology or process thinkers, and has probably discouraged others from entering this thicket. Hence the long delay in the emergence of process Christologies. Thornton's example had to be forgotten before others would venture forth with their own proposals.

Thornton did not intend to write a Whiteheadian Christology, although that is what many who read him were looking for. He is primarily a church theologian presenting a high Christology in conversation with Whitehead's analysis of experience. He is decidedly not a process theist: "As long as there is genuine religious experience remaining, the religious attitude will never give up its treasured truth that God is the eternal and unchanging Creator, who utterly transcends the changing drama of this present world and all that it contains."[1] Nevertheless he was an enthusiastic Whiteheadian, profoundly influenced by Whitehead's philosophy of nature. This was still possible in 1928, for the dynamic, temporal character of God's consequent nature was first introduced in *Process and Reality* (1929). At the time Thornton had closely read *The Concept of Nature* (1920) and *Principles of Natural Knowledge* (2d edition, 1925), tended to interpret *Science and the Modern World* (1925) in line with these earlier works, and was acquainted with *Religion in the Making* (1926) though somewhat unsure what to make of its doctrine of God.[2] He took comfort in Whitehead's remark concerning the immortality of the soul, and evidently wanted to apply it to all theological issues: "There is no reason why such a question should not be decided on more special evidence, religious or otherwise, provided that it is trustworthy."[3] Whitehead's proposal to develop a strictly metaphysical concept of God with secular functions was not picked up.

Thornton was attracted by Whitehead's evolutionary conceptions of nature, and particularly by his dissolution of scientific materialism into organic events. Especially in his earlier writings (including the earlier sections of *Science and the Modern World*), Whitehead develops a theory of overlapping events characterized by reiterated patterns, showing how sub-events may be organically influenced by the patterns of the events within which they are included. Such influence modifies and transforms simpler organisms into component elements of more complex organisms, thereby allowing for evolutionary growth.[4] From this Thornton develops a hierarchy of stages: matter, life, mind, and spirit, each as a new emergent from its predecessor.

Yet the doctrine of real emergence in nature is balanced by an awareness of the ancient principle *ex nihilo nihil fit*: "The new cannot properly speaking emerge out of an existing situation. It may appear as thus emerging; but it must enter from beyond . . . . What cannot emerge out of the process of events in the series enters into that series from beyond it, that is, from the eternal order."[5] This is a remarkable anticipation of Whitehead's view in *Process and Reality* that God's primordial ordering of the world's possibilities (the eternal objects) is the ultimate source of novelty in an emergent universe, except that Thornton understands these possibilities to be everlasting rather than timeless.[6] This reification of what for Whitehead is purely possible, needing concrete embodiment in the actual world, leads Thornton to conceive of the eternal order as absolutely actual in its unchangeableness, identical with God. Then the world becomes an unnecessary appendage to God, a strange reduplication in time of that which is already unchangingly actual in God. The reciprocal interplay and mutual dependence between God and the world, so characteristic of Whitehead, are here absent. Like Hartshorne, Thornton argues that God is essentially self-giving love which must find expression in another, but he uses this argument not to establish the necessity of creation, but to demonstrate the existence of a social trinity of interacting persons.[7] This Trinitarianism, moreover, leads to an interesting identification of two of Whitehead's formative elements in the creation of actual entities, the realm of eternal objects and creativity, with the second and third persons of the Trinity respectively.[8]

Nevertheless, given these principles, Thornton could have devised an evolutionary Christology such that God's creative Word, already manifest in each emergent process, has been decisively actualized for man in Jesus of Nazareth. The man Jesus could then be the bearer of that divine activity carrying man beyond himself. Such a view would have been a consistent development of the process interpretation adopted in the first half of the book, integrating both man and the divine activity in the world into the total process of nature. But Thornton can envisage no evolutionary advance beyond man,[9] and sees in spirit, the distinctively human characteristic, primarily an openness and receptivity (when not thwarted by sin) to the eternal order. This in turn is tied to a concept of God as "Absolute Actuality" which is the identification of universality with concrete individuality.[10] Apparently relying here on F. H. Bradley's concrete universal, Thornton conceives of divine individuality as an all-embracing unity, and it is this principle of unity which must be incarnate in Christ. Since this divine individuality cannot be gradually introduced into the creative process, that process cannot be allowed to progressively culminate in the

Christ, but must be seen merely as the material basis for the sudden irruption of the Logos-Creator from beyond. "Each stage in the incorporation of creative activity produced a new level of the series. But the Eternal Word is very God. His self-incorporation into the organic series does not, therefore, constitute a new level of the old series."[11] "The Incarnation brings creation to its true end in God,"[12] which constitutes a new creation decisively different from the old creation in gradual evolution. "The Christ whom Christians worship as God is not a product of creative activity . . . . not simply the projection and continuation of the curve of ascent which marks the pathway of creative activity in its incorporation into the organic series,"[13] but the descent of God from beyond.

From the standpoint of process thought, this conception of the incarnation presupposes a self-sufficient creator who need not seek fulfillment in creaturely actualization and whose incorporation within the world is wholly discontinuous with its ongoing process. It is strikingly similar to the traditional Catholic doctrine of a divinely infused soul into the first man Adam, who otherwise may be understood as the product of the evolution of the primates, and bristles with the sharp dualisms between creator and creature which process theism has sought to overcome. Norman Pittenger,[14] Charles E. Raven,[15] and Dorothy Emmet[16] have criticized Thornton on this score.

Quite apart from these concerns, students of Christology have objected to the implication of Thornton's argument that Christ's individuality must be divine rather than human. Thornton's defense against the charge that he denies Christ's humanity is not wholly convincing:

> We have not to search, as some have supposed, for a central core which must be abstracted to make room for the eternal Logos. All the principles of unity which exist in any other human organism exist also in Him. But whereas in created human beings the highest law of being [= the principle of individuality] is that transcending principle of unity which is proper to a human organism, . . . the highest law of being in His case is the law of being proper to deity. . . . The human body is not less physical because it is taken up into a spiritual organism and has become an organ of spirit. Neither is the human organism less human because it is taken up into union with the eternal Logos and has become the organ of His deity.[17]

This overlooks the fact that each new principle of individuality creates a new species, and Christ is here depicted as belonging to a different species from man. Christ is both divine and human on Thornton's account in the same way that man is both human and animal.[18] Jesus cannot be one with us in our humanity unless he is also a man, not a divine being who subsumes humanity within himself.

We may generalize the issues raised by Thornton's proposal by asking whether any high Christology is possible within a process perspective. Is it possible for the divine subjectivity to become actualized in some way within the man Jesus? Our answer is negative, for none of the alternatives seem to work. Either we adopt a social trinity in which only one of several divine subjectivities becomes incarnate, or the one and only subjectivity of God is realized in Jesus. But a social trinity is impossible on Whitehead's terms, since "person" in the sense of an individual center of subjectivity must be identified with "substance" as the underlying unity of an actuality. For the unity of an actual entity in its process of coming to be is precisely its unification or growth together (concrescence), which is its subjectivity as experienced from within. Subjectivity and substantial unity cannot be displaced from one another, so the time-honored formula, *una substantia in tres personae* collapses unless "persona" is understood rather as an abstract aspect or mode of activity of a single concrete subjectivity. If that single divine subjectivity is realized in Jesus, then either not all of God is taken up in Christ, or Christ is identified with the totality of God, or God is in some sense diminished or altered in Christ. The first possibility would treat God the Father or the Godhead as some sort of vacuous actuality devoid of subjectivity; at any rate it would, like the second possibility, ascribe all divine subjective attributes to the subjectivity of Jesus (who can only have one unified subjectivity, not one divine and one human), which is both implausible and heretical. If to avoid such doceticism we adopt the radical kenoticism of Thomas Altizer, accepting a successive trinity such that in Christ God (the Father) died to be received by us as wholly immanent Spirit, then we must explain how universally necessary divine attributes (such as God's full experience of every actuality) can have such an abrupt and contingent end.

None of the process Christologies we have examined propose that the divine subjectivity has become actualized within the man Jesus; rather, they contend that God was in Christ objectively, the way any actuality can be present in another according to Whitehead's principles, though with considerably more profundity and richness. J. E. Barnhart comes the closest to articulating the concerns of high Christology as to how God could become man in Christ.[19] "Through empathy with the man Jesus, God did become not a *man* but, rather, became *human*. By 'identifying' with Jesus, God experienced certain *human* predicates, especially singular *care* for a dearly beloved and the *dread* of being estranged from him."[20] God could not become a man without thereby abandoning his divinity (as in Altizer's Sabellianism), but he becomes fully human in intimately incorporating into his own being peculiarly human experiences and sensitivities, thus accepting an inexhaustible concern for human purposes, achievements, and failures. But in this sense God became human not with Christ but with Adam. "The primordial divine will-to-experience-humanity," which Barnhart identifies with the "potential Christ in God"[21] becomes actualized within God with the first emergence of man. It is true that "in the historical Jesus, God's will-to-value-and-fellowship"[22] met a special fulfillment in a peculiar, reciprocal intensification of mutual involvement, but this in itself is not the way God became human, although from a human perspective it may make accessible to us the richness of God's concern for us. Christology cannot be the locus for God's becoming human, although it may reveal to us the depth of his humanity for us.

The stubborn, persistent problem of classical Christology, how one person could be both fully divine and fully human, practically disappears within a Whiteheadian framework. In that framework events and activities are primary, while enduring substantial personhood is derivative. No concrete, actual event, moreover, can be understood as either wholly the work of God or the work of man (or of any other creature). Each event requires the persuasive power of God to provide the lure or possibility or initial aim to be realized, but it also requires the creaturely power to actualize that aim by integrating together the totality of efficient causes derived from the past. Without God there would be simply chaos, for the individual occasion would lack any ordering principle to initiate its process of integration, but without the world, God's aims for the world would never be realized, since God acts solely by the power of persuasion, which can be effective only so far as it elicits concrete response. This means that *every* creaturely activity is also a divine activity, incarnating God's purposes in the world, to greater or lesser degree. Only those actions which are fully responsive to God's aims, to be sure, *reveal* God's action in the world, for only they realize his intentions without distortion.

Other events may thwart or frustrate or only partially realize the divine intent, but they still necessarily involve divine action, though with diminished effectiveness. "The world lives by its incarnation of God in itself."[23]

Whitehead's recognition of this incarnational universe is implicit in his high praise for "the schools of thought mainly associated with Alexandria and Antioch . . . . These Christian theologians have the distinction of being the only thinkers who in a fundamental metaphysical doctrine have improved upon Plato . . . . They pointed out the way in which Platonic metaphysics should develop, if it was to give a rational account of the role of the persuasive agency of God."[24] For Plato, the world can only contain copies or images or imitations of God and the Ideas which he contemplates. The Nicene fathers were faced with the problem of understanding how God could be present in Christ. "On this topic, there can be no doubt that the Arian solution, involving a derivative Image, is orthodox Platonism, though it be heterodox Christianity."[25] In contrast the church fathers decided for the direct immanence of God in the world, restricting its application to the one instance of the person of Christ. For all of their advance on Plato, these theologians failed to generalize their results because of an unfortunate presupposition: "The nature of God was exempted from all the metaphysical categories which applied to the individual things in the temporal world. . . . They made no effort to conceive the World in terms of the metaphysical categories by means of which they interpreted God, and they made no effort to conceive God in terms of the metaphysical categories which they applied to the World."[26] Whitehead does, and hence conceives of the Platonic Ideas (his "eternal objects") as directly immanent in each actual occasion as the means whereby God's directing activity is really present in every creature. In a world where every actuality incarnates God, even if in a very diminished way, the christological problem must be put quite differently: what is the special characteristic of general human significance defining a Christ-event, enabling Christians to confess that they find it decisively realized in Jesus of Nazareth?

Since the degree to which God's aims are incarnated depends upon the quality of creaturely response, it is not surprising that some process thinkers such as Norman Pittenger, Peter Hamilton, and Ronald Williams have taken Jesus' total obedience to God as the clue to the specialness of the Christ-event.[27] This criterion, however, is entirely too general to describe the specific characteristics which ought to pertain to the Christ. It only describes "sinlessness" or "creaturely perfection" or "saintliness." The Christ may well have all these properties, but are they sufficiently distinctive to single him out from amid a host of other good and holy persons? Complete human response to the divine prompting may be a necessary but not a sufficient condition for the Christ-event if we define such response in relative rather than absolute terms. There is creaturely perfection wherever there is optimal achievement of value, *given* the antecedent causal conditions that creature unifies in its actualization.

Once we take into account the crucial role such antecedent conditions play, we see that there are as many different kinds of possible optimal achievements for persons as there are different situations confronting them. At every moment in our lives we have the opportunity of achieving the maximum value potentially inherent in each situation, but should such optimal realization be classed forthwith as "Christ-events"? The question may be put historically: could Socrates, as a fourth-century Athenian, possibly have become the Christ? Not if our understanding of what the Christ is presupposes in any way the historical circumstance of Israel's expectation of a coming Messiah. If all such historical conditions, on the other hand, can be systematically ignored as irrelevant, it becomes highly problematic on what grounds we award the title of Christ to Jesus and yet continue to withhold it from Socrates or from Gautama.

Let us then specify "Christ-events" as one particular species of human events characterized by the successful achievement of "christological aims," as yet unspecified as to content. In this fashion we may readily grant that Socrates and Gautama and any number of saints or just plain good people have frequently achieved the maximum value possible in given situations without thereby claiming them to be Christs, on the grounds that the aims they so richly actualized were not specifically christological. Such christological aims depend upon the grace of God, and he bestows them on some and not on others. Nevertheless, God's activity is not arbitrary, since he inexorably seeks the best possible aims appropriate to the circumstances. It is only in certain special situations, however, that these specific aims can embody christological aims.

In *A Process Christology,* David R. Griffin notes the same difficulties we have raised about these proposals: "They have not made use of the notion that the content of God's ideal aims for men varies. . . .If this notion of Whitehead's is not used, the resulting Christology has a somewhat Pelagian quality, suggesting that Jesus' specialness is due solely to human initative—if Jesus was God's decisive revelation, this did not result even partially from any special activity on God's part in any sense."[28]

Griffin therefore focuses his attention upon what we have called the christological aim, although he generalizes it beyond the scope of mankind: "In actualizing God's *particular* aims *for him*, Jesus expressed God's *general* aim for his entire creation."[29] This generalization is possible because of the specific content he assigns to the christological aim: "The aims given to Jesus and actualized by him during his active ministry were such that the basic vision of reality contained in his message of work and deed was the supreme expression of God's eternal character and purpose."[30]

Clearly the event of Christ does reveal to us the personal character of God. Christians have seen, and will continue to see in Jesus as the Christ the supreme revelation of God's personhood. Surely Griffin's position is sound to this extent. Nevertheless, we do not feel that he has made full use of the resources available in process theism when he restricts what is revealed in Christ to the eternal essence of God. In classical theism, which insists upon God's simplicity, immutability, and eternality, the eternal essence of God was all that could possibly be revealed of God. Process theism, on the other hand, makes a formal distinction between God's abstract, necessary essence and its concrete, contingent embodiment which is responsive to the vicissitudes of the world. Griffin stresses that this contingent dimension is necessarily involved in God's provision of initial aims, including those which express the special christological aim, since the content of such aims is constantly changing, contingent on circumstance. Clearly there is also additional contingent content in the special aims for Jesus' life which accompany and embody the christological aim for Griffin, but these are dismissed as only of historical significance. They are relevant only to the particularities of those occasions which gave rise to the supreme revelation of God. Doubtless many aspects of those complex special aims have little systematic import. Yet a third factor may be present in these aims, a contingent component distinct from the eternal aim which, nevertheless, may have significance for the entire human situation.

God's personal character is revealed in the contingencies of his particular dealings with his creatures. Insofar as God has an eternal, permanent essence, this is exemplified in every interaction where there is an adequate response to God. This is the character of God's general revelation, and is fully accessible to metaphysical investigation. Theology's focus, in contrast, should concern the special, contingent dimension of God's personal relationship to the human situation. Humanity is a contingent species, which need never have existed. If so, the special character of God's salvific action on man's behalf must also be contingent. This means that theology has its own intrinsic subject matter, since this contingent dimension can never be discovered by metaphysical analysis, but must await historical disclosure. Metaphysics reveals what God is like *for all creatures*, as Hartshorne tells us, but religion makes manifest what God is like *for us*. In our religious faith we are not primarily concerned with the univeral character of God's loving response. We are concerned with the specific way that loving response is directed toward us in our own particular existential predicament. This can only be revealed in contingent historical particularities.

"In actualizing God's *particular* aims *for him*," Griffin assures us, "Jesus expressed God's *general* aim for his entire creation."[31] We agree, but insist that this is too abstract and general for the purposes of theology. Theology is properly concerned with God's *specific* aim for mankind. Since this specific aim must be contingent, it can only be discovered if historically revealed.

This distinction becomes all the more important once we place Christology within the context of possible intelligent life elsewhere in the universe. In Christ God has become incarnate as man, and for man, but is he thereby incarnate for other forms of intelligent life as well? Previously this question could be dismissed as idle speculation, but since the Second World War, there has been a dramatic upsurge of interest in life on other worlds. For many people, particularly those engaged in the natural sciences, the notion of extraterrestrial life is no longer merely an exotic possibility but a virtual certainty. The issue chiefly turns on our confidence in the regularity of planetary development and of evolutionary growth. If both of these occur regularly, spontaneously, then we should expect the universe to be populated with myriads of planets sustaining life, many of which could be technical civilizations far in advance of ours. On the other hand, if the origin of life, or the formation of planets, is a chance, freak occurrence, then we may well be alone in the universe.

Both views of planetary development have been with us for a long time. The French naturalist Georges de Buffon (1707–1788) proposed that the birth of the planets resulted from a glancing collision of our sun with a passing comet. In contrast, Immanuel Kant and Pierre de Laplace argued that planetary development was part of a normal process to be expected in the life of almost every star: they assumed the young sun was surrounded by a thin lens-shaped gaseous envelope (solar nebula) which later condensed into planets. During the late nineteenth century the Kant-Laplace hypothesis was severely criticized by the British physicist Clerk Maxwell, who argued that the forces of differential rotation between parts of the solar nebula would break up any such condensation as soon as it began to form. In the face of this objection, which seemed quite decisive at the time, cosmologists increasingly turned to some version of Buffon's glancing collision. Forest Ray Moulton and Thomas C. Chamberlin in the United States supposed that the sun, under the gravitational pull of some passing star, erupted gigantic globs of matter which in time formed planets, and a comparable theory was proposed by Sir James Jeans and H. Jeffreys. Yet the collisions or near misses dictated by these theories are inherently very improbable, perhaps only ten for the entire life of our galaxy during the past five billion years.[32] With so few planets in existence, we could hardly assume that there would be much life elsewhere, at least not in our galaxy.

Both types of theories developed difficulties, but Maxwell's objections to the Kant-Laplace hypothesis were overcome toward the end of World War II by C. F. von Weizsäcker, who argued that the original objections were based on the assumption that the chemical composition of the sun resembled that of the earth. We now know that the heavier, terrestrial elements compose less than one per cent of the sun's mass, the rest being essentially a mixture of the two lightest elements, hydrogen and helium. Von Weizsäcker argued for a differential treatment between the hydrogen-helium and heavier elements with respect to the angular momentum of original solar mass. With the issue thus resolved in favor of a regular formation of planets, the chance of there being other planets capable of sustaining life is so high as to be practically certain. Even if only one planet out of every 150,000 contained life, there would be one million life-worlds in our galaxy, some of which we can reasonably assume contain intelligent life, for whom, we presume, God would also be concerned.

As Paul Tillich has seen:

> . . .a question arises which has been carefully avoided by many traditional theologians, even though it is consciously or unconsciously alive for most contemporary people. It is the problem of how to understand the meaning of the symbol "Christ" (or any other man-centered religious symbol, for that matter) in the light of the immensity of the universe, the heliocentric system of planets, the infinitely small part of the universe which man and his history constitute, and the possibility of other "worlds" in which divine self-manifestations may appear and be received.[33]

Now what can we say about God's relation to such intelligent beings on other planets? Here our approach cannot be existential, for we cannot participate in the self-understanding such beings might possess, nor can our reflections significantly influence, or be derived from, our own quest for a meaningful selfhood. The issue is quite theoretical, but it is one which helps us to see the boundaries and implications of one particular faith-stance in the wider context of others. Christian thinkers have reflected on these boundaries with respect to their fellow human beings in other cultures, and even with respect to the other animals which share our planet, but rarely with respect to the rest of life populating the universe.

Moreover, the issue entails cosmological assertions bearing on our scientific understanding of the universe. For we must show the possibility of God's involvement in the emergence of other forms of intelligent life before any claim can be entertained concerning their existential standing before God, and this task invites dialogue with scientific accounts of evolutionary processes.

While it may not express itself in these terms, the scientific community has become increasingly confident in the tremendous potential inherent in the universe for evolutionary growth. If the proper conditions are present, for example, surface temperatures permitting large bodies of liquid such as water or ammonia or methane, atmospheres permitting of energy-exchange, some source of light, etc., most scientists expect that sooner or later life will emerge. The extreme resiliency and bouyancy of the evolutionary thrust make it unlikely that, if all necessary environmental conditions are met, prebiotic molecules will not eventually emerge to be followed by some form of life.

In 1953, Stanley L. Miller, a collaborator of Harold C. Urey at the University of Chicago, prepared a mixture of methane, ammonia, and water vapor in simulation of the primitive atmosphere postulated for the earth. Stimulated by an electrode discharge passing through the mixture, within a week it yielded a variety of organic molecules: amino acids, acetic acid, simple sugars. Some of these are the building blocks used in the formation of living cells. If such dramatic growth was possible in such a short interval of time, under the proper conditions we can expect the same sort of process to occur on other worlds. This does not mean to imply that precisely these organic compounds must first be synthesized in order to allow life to emerge, but that these could have been the compounds used here on earth for the formation of life. On other worlds it is conceivable that an original atmosphere rich in hydrogen cyanide would have produced other organic building blocks. We anticipate some sort of growth toward increased complexity: increasingly larger organic macro-molecules, then the convergence of many macromolecules to constitute a simple living system, either as a cell with its protective wall and vital nucleus or as some functional analogue, then the convergence of many cells to form larger organisms.

Since Darwin, this process of evolutionary growth, whereby levels of increasing complexity are seen to emerge from simpler ones, has been explained in terms of the double mechanism of natural selection and chance variation. Natural selection affords a measure of stability and durability, for those populations which happen to be best adapted to their environments continue to survive as other populations tend to die out. By itself, however, natural selection provides for no evolutionary advance, for it introduces no novelty, and hence no possibility of anything more than that which already has been. We must recognize that in this context "adaptation" is strictly defined in terms of survival values and that, generally speaking, it is the simpler forms of organization that possess the greatest staying power: living systems, no matter how fantastically intricate and well organized they might be, have a much shorter span of existence than, say, a rock crystal, or a single stable atom.[34]

The stability of natural selection must be balanced by the novelty of chance variation, which permits the introduction of new forms of existence. In principle this is as far as a scientific explanation can go if it proceeds by strict limitation to efficient causal explanation. Seen most broadly, any efficient causal explanation restricts itself to that which is traditional, for it explains the present in terms of the past. Efficient causality is the way in which the past persists into the present, and the task of scientific analysis is to discover whatever regularity exists in this transfer from past to present. Everything that happens either follows regularly established patterns or just happens quite accidentally. Ultimately, then, regularity and chance are our only options, and chance signifies little more than the absence of scientific causal explanation. Yet, without chance, nothing new could ever occur, that is, new in the sense of establishing novel causal patterns and forms of organization. If everything happened strictly according to deterministic physical laws, there would be no possibility for the emergence of life, if one assumes that the organization of life, while dependent upon physical principles, is not reducible to them. Fortunately, physical laws are probabilistic, with an indeterminacy that permits the emergence of novelty. Without chance, there can be no evolutionary advance, yet, strictly speaking, chance explains nothing. It is merely the absence of any efficient causal explanation.

Now the evolutionary process is essentially the emergence of new levels of complexity. Given the character of scientific explanation in terms of efficient causes, it is quite understandable that such evolutionary advance should be explained in terms of natural selection and chance variation as the best possible scientific theory. Chance supplies the novelty, while natural selection permits the consolidation of gains. Nevertheless, as an account of the whole story, it is quite incredible.

Essentially, what is lacking is any account as to why new levels of complexity should ever be achieved. Chance variation will produce novel forms of organization which may be more or less complex than that which preceded it. But should there be any greater tendency for the more complex rather than for the less complex to persist from such variation? Random activity should actually tend to favor the less complex for three reasons. (1) The simpler depends upon fewer specific conditions and has fewer, less demanding needs; human life, for example, depends upon so many more factors than single-celled marine life does. (2) The less complex is more in accord with entropy, the principle that any closed system tends to decrease in order over time. (3) With time, the possibility that random variation should produce anything with greater order should decrease as entropy increases.

God's cosmological function consists in supplying that impetus toward greater complexification that we discover to be operative throughout the natural order. This does not mean that God acts efficiently as one of the causal antecedent conditions out of which the present event emerges. Rather he serves as a lure for actualization, providing novel possibilities of achievement. Persuasion entails response, not conformation, and the response is free either to embrace or to reject the novel aim. We do not mean to suggest that there is much free response in the universe: atoms and molecules are extremely traditional in their habits, behaving largely as they have always behaved. Plants, animals, and even humans are not much better, blindly reiterating that which went on before. Yet if there is to be any emergence of greater complexity, then there must be at least a modicum of spontaneous response possible even on the atomic and molecular levels, occasionally permitting the actualization of some evolutionary advance. Divine persuasion is the urge to maximize the possibilities inherent in such indeterminate response.

In a very real sense this theory of divine initiative and creaturely response commits us to some form of neo-Lamarckianism, for we are affirming that the inheritance of acquired characteristics is fundamental to evolutionary advance. In appropriating the divine possibility as its own aim, the creature is acquiring some characteristic which is then transmitted by means of efficient causality to subsequent generations. Free response becomes blind habit; novelty becomes tradition; final causality passes over into efficient causality. As we have noted, the realm of activity not wholly governed by efficient causal patterns may be vanishingly small on the simplest levels of existence, but that quantitatively negligible amount is all important in furthering any increased complexity. Random mutation is incapable of explaining the directedness of evolution such response can introduce. Once introduced, however, the new characteristic may be simply transmitted through blind habit.[35]

Generally speaking neo-Lamarckianism, as usually understood, has been properly discredited, but for the wrong reasons. It is not the inheritance of acquired characteristics which is erroneous, but the failure to distinguish properly between "levels" of response. How a given person or animal responds to his environmental situation will not affect the genetic makeup of his descendants, for that genetic makeup is determined on the cellular, perhaps even on the molecular level. If sufficiently original, human response may shape the common culture inherited by our fellows, for every tradition blindly received originally had its purpose and justification, however feeble that might have been. But if we restrict ourselves to biological inheritance, then we must examine cellular and molecular response, ignoring all higher responses on the level of the total organism. Here we can only conjecture, for it is difficult to appreciate what aims DNA molecules may strive to actualize. It may be doubted, however, that such aims would embrace even the relevant aims of the cell to which the DNA molecules belong, let alone the aims of the total animal body. Precisely in this sense, we can say that any gene mutations introduced by novel actualizations by such DNA molecules are random with regard to the future of the total organism in much the same way that the realization of our personal goals is usually random with respect to the future of the human race as a whole.[36]

Creaturely response through the appropriation of a novel aim supplied by God, on whatever level, whether atomic, molecular, cellular, or organismic, becomes the chief means whereby divine purposes become effective in the world. This does not mean, however, that the created order proceeds according to some set plan. Divine persuasion is highly opportunistic, seeking to maximize possibilities for increasing complexity which are consistent with the actual conditions imposed by the past through efficient causation. Moreover, this persuasion is not coercive, so there is no necessity that every creature must embody the maximum of its potentialities. Whatever happens, happens as the result of the creature's self-activity in utilizing its causal conditions to achieve its ends, but God is everywhere and at all times seeking that which is best, given the circumstances. Such gracious activity will not always be thwarted, so that evolutionary advance, as actualized through free creaturely response, gradually comes into being.

Thus, for the universe at large, divine persuasion seeks to evoke life wherever possible, in the form appropriate to particular local conditions. We assume that there are common physical laws for the entire observable universe, and these laws yield universal laws of chemical bonding. We can be reasonably certain that the way molecules are formed is invariant throughout the universe, and that the most promising chemical elements for organic evolution will be the lighter elements toward the center of the periodic table capable of very supple and complex co-valent bonding.

From this point on, however, the evolutionary process may branch in many directions, for the macromolecules formed out of these elements will vary considerably depending upon the composition and distribution of such elements in the early stages of that world. One-celled microorganisms, in developing their metabolism, will depend in turn upon whatever macromolecules are available, so we should expect every world to have its own way of organizing simple living systems. As we know from the past history of evolution on this earth, the development of multicelled organisms with or without central coordination (that is, animals and plants) can take many different routes, but these routes might be even more varied if the basic cellular structure were also radically different. The possibilities are naturally enormous.

The increase of freedom may be a divine purpose appropriate to all worlds. Freedom is essentially self-creation, requiring both the absence of restraint and the introduction of order by the free agent. On the atomic and molecular level there is a minimum of spontaneity, for each response is overwhelmingly the product of blind habit, endlessly reiterating the same pattern of activity it has inherited. We may think of molecules as societies of atoms, and molecules have been discovered to have preserved their structures intact for a good billion years. The decisive difference between living and lifeless matter, as Whitehead saw, is the difference between novel and habitual response. This may be a matter of degree, such that what we designate as living may simply be those instances where novelty dominates over habit. Homeostatic adjustment within the living cell requires that it respond to its surroundings in original ways which supersede the customary behavior of molecules.

At a higher level, motility frees animals from spatial confinement and renders them open to a great variety of situations to respond to. Yet without sentience, such motility would simply lead to random behavior; sight and smell and touch enable animals to achieve purposeful results meaningful to them. Intelligence is simply the next step in the quest for greater freedom; imagination increases our field of action by including the possible as well as the actual, while reason enables us to order these possibilities in significant ways.

As the capacity for novelty expands, consciousness emerges. We cannot define consciousness in terms of a centralized nervous system, for there is a great deal of neurological activity lying below the threshold of consciousness. Habitual patterns of response, such as getting dressed, riding a bicycle, using a typewriter, so painfully and self-consciously learned at the time, become quite unconscious.[37] A centralized nervous system or its close analogue may be the necessary basis for consciousness, but consciousness itself is the inner concomitant of the presence of some novelty which has not yet faded into the background through incessant repetition.

Once intelligence appears, cultures may develop, varying enormously among themselves, but sharing the common biological inheritance and common general environment for that planet. Thus we should expect cultural differentiation on other worlds, but despite their diversity all would be characteristically stamped by that biological situation, just as all our cultures by contrast will be found to have certain peculiarly "terrestrial" features. We may leave open the question whether intelligent cultures must further develop into technical civilizations, that is, into civilizations seeking to transform environmental conditions to suit their own purposes and needs. It may be that human technology is essentially an accident owing to the fact that man is biologically so poorly adapted to his natural surroundings. It is quite possible, for example, that the dolphins possess a highly refined culture transmitted orally from generation to generation, but that they have developed no technology because they have no need of it. Man is a tool-using animal, but it may not be necessary that all intelligent species must also become tool-using.

With the emergence of conscious alternatives of action, ethics becomes possible, for now some options may be experienced as better and others as worse. What goodness means for other intelligent beings may well be beyond the bounds of our imagination, but it might be just possible to define a general criterion underlying all concrete embodiments. That which fosters the expansion of freedom and the intensity of experience may be regarded as good, although the ways in which freedom and intensity are fostered will depend upon the biological, psychological, social, cultural, political, economic, and possibly religious situations in which particular intelligent beings find themselves.

Throughout this multifarious universe the divine creativity is operative, evoking greater and greater levels of complexity, thereby permitting the expansion of freedom and the emergence of intense conscious experience. With consciousness it becomes possible for creatures to be aware of

God's directing activity, although on earth this seems to be generally rather sporadic and intermittent. In general the basic way in which God acts on the human level is through ethical persuasion; it is by the worthiness, the attractiveness, the importance of specific ethical ends envisioned that God lures us on to actualize a world better than what we have known. Such divine persuasion can be effective wherever man is willing to be ethically sensitive, quite apart from whether he consciously affirms or denies the existence of such divine reality. In this context, we may define God as that dynamic source of values which lures the evolutionary process to an ever-richer complexity productive of increasing freedom and intensity of experience. As such, God is necessarily operative in the development of every life and in every culture, whether terrestrial or extraterrestrial.

Now in terms of these speculations, is it possible for us to do justice to the Christian claim that God acted decisively in Jesus of Nazareth for the salvation of all mankind? We have sketched a liberal theology for the cosmos, but is it also appropriate for our existence here and now? Or need we surrender the claim of Christ's decisiveness in the name of some unproven conjecture?

John bears witness that the Logos of God, by which he created the world, became flesh and dwelt among us. Are we then to conclude that God's only Son became uniquely incarnate once and for all on the third planet of a rather ordinary outlying star of a thoroughly undistinguished galaxy? Paul Tillich argues to the contrary: "Incarnation is unique for the special group in which it happens, but it is not unique in the sense that other singular incarnations for other unique worlds are excluded. Man, cannot claim to occupy the only possible place for Incarnation."[38] Accordingly, we find it useful to make a distinction ignored by our forefathers in the naive assumption of the uniqueness and exalted status of man. We understand by the Logos or divine creative Word the sum totality of all God's specific creative purposes for all creatures. The Word or speech of God symbolized the divine activity whereby new structural possibilities for the emergence of greater complexity become lures of feeling for further actualization. Yet this creative purpose is hardly invariant in its specific manifestations: what God says depends upon the particular situation confronting that individual in his own world. The speech appropriate to macromolecules capable of converging to form the nucleus of a living cell is characteristically different from the ethical imperative addressing twentieth-century Americans. Both differ sharply from that Word addressing intelligent creatures who may dwell in some super-civilization centuries ahead of our own. God's dynamic Word knows no single form, but assumes that character expressive of God's general aim at intensity of experience appropriate to each circumstance. By this Word the worlds were created, and by this Word also God has sought the salvation of his people, Israel.

The Logos, then, refers to the totality of God's creative aims. We may distinguish this from the Christ, which signifies that one specific divine creative purpose addressed to the human situation, designed to bring about our salvation. To affirm that Jesus is the Christ is to confess that in Jesus of Nazareth we behold the embodiment of the divine intent addressed to mankind. The Word appropriate to our condition becomes incarnate by becoming fully actualized in the words, deeds, and suffering of Jesus. God has spoken before and since to man, with fragmentary success; his Word has come down again and again, but never before has it so taken root and become flesh. For it must be recognized that the divine Word depends upon creaturely response for its actualization. All of God's urging will do no good unless we act; but then again, we would not be inclined to act at all unless our ethical and religious sensibilities were aroused by God's prompting.

In Christ we have the promise of God's salvation for all people, but what does this salvation mean? When the aged Simeon beheld the Christ child who would save his people from their sins, he probably understood the liberation of Israel from Roman oppression, the consequence of the people's sin against their God. Paul then took this common formula, and transformed the meaning of salvation, so that we are being saved from the sins themselves and not merely from their consequences. In its deepest sense, salvation is that which overcomes our guilt, meaninglessness, and alienation from the creative source of all value, that which saves us from ultimate futility.

Salvation is the application of God's creative purpose to intelligent life. Everywhere God's creative urging toward the establishment of increased levels of intensity is present, but only with intelligent life can there be any awareness of this. At the same time, only with intelligent life can there be any sense of alienation from divine creativity, any awareness of our capacity to thwart the divine purpose by self-centered activities randomly conflicting with one another. As the only apparently intelligent creature on earth, man can sense the meaninglessness of his life apart from God. Even though the individual life may be cherished by God forever, its purposes by itself are ridiculously puny. But the individual need not experience his life in and of itself, but as participating in the broad sweep of divine creation, contributing in its small way to the increased intensification of divine experience, making possible the emergence of new forms of existence beyond man. We shall consider what one of these newly emergent forms might be in the next chapter. Here it is important to appreciate the intimate connection between salvation and creation. Creation in the sense of the emergence of levels of intensification in concert with divine persuasion is universal, and the salvation of each (intelligent) level depends upon its participation in the creation of the next higher level. For creation is the ultimate, all-inclusive context of meaning and value in terms of which we can be saved.

Jesus as the Christ is the incarnation of God's dynamic Word addressed to us as confessing Christians, but should we say that he is the only incarnation for mankind? If we think of incarnation primarily in terms of the actualization of the divine creative purpose creating that which takes us beyond man, we may be tempted to reply affirmatively. But John Cobb, addressing himself to just this problem in *Christ in a Pluralistic Age*, is teaching some of us to consider "incarnation" in an additional, more extended meaning. Here "incarnation" does not refer so much to the *actualization* as to the *embodiment* of divine aims in the lives of people, whereby the very abstract aims conceptually entertained in God's primordial experience are transformed into concrete possibilities or effective lures for our action and self-understanding. In this sense God is incarnated in every religious tradition through every image or symbol which effectively expresses its deepest response to God's leading, although the Christian can confess that for him Christ, the incarnation of God, is supremely exemplified in Jesus.

This may be an idiosyncratic reading of *Christ in a Pluralistic Age*,[39] yet it follows naturally from Cobb's proposal that Christ should be accorded the status of a Whiteheadian proposition.[40] Such a proposition is neither an actuality nor a pure possibility but a hybrid of both. It functions normally as real or concrete possibility for the future, sharing with the pure primordial possibilities their unactualized status, yet being also rooted in the actualities of the past which form the causal conditions by which it could someday become actual. Pure possibilities as such are irrelevant to the ongoing course of the temporal world. They must first become "incarnate" in the sense of becoming interwoven with the concrete vicissitudes of historical circumstance in order to become effective lures for the future. Only those possibilities which are realizable under present circumstances (or which may shortly become realizable) are live options for future actualization. The divine Logos, as the primordial mind of God, contains an infinity of pure possibility, but only those possibilities specifically addressed to the human situation can save us. These possibilities are addressed to our situation by becoming incarnate in our living religious traditions, which clothe abstract divine aims with the symbolic imagery which speaks to our concrete needs.

As St. Ambrose has said, it is not by dialectic that God has been pleased to save his people.[41] Pure abstract concepts have no saving significance. Religious symbols, not concepts, mediate to us the divine. These symbols are rooted in historical circumstance, not human contrivance; they are "born," "live," and "die" within the life of the communities shaped by them. We must be wary of reducing the symbols of other traditions to the bare concepts they embody. This may enable us to understand them in terms of our own conceptualities, but it robs them of their particular salvific power. If we see that the very generation of such effective concrete lures is the *incarnation* (in this extended sense) of divine aims, then there is a deeply Christian reason for affirming the positive valuations of other traditions on their own terms.

While Cobb's proposals about "incarnation" address the problem of the pluralism of faiths in a most exciting manner, we have deep reservations about his analysis of incarnation in the more usual, restricted sense as applying to how Jesus can be the Christ. For Jesus' specific individuality, Cobb suggests that the center of his subjectivity is co-constituted by the divine Logos, understood as the unity of the ideals, aims, and possibilities that God cherishes for the world. This theme was first announced in "A Whiteheadian Christology,"[42] and here it is carefully developed in terms of the peculiar authority Jesus claimed which contemporary witnesses attested to according to recent New Testament scholars as diverse as Rudolf Bultmann, Norman Perrin, Ernest C. Colwell, and

Milan Machoveč. Jesus may well have possessed this peculiar authority, but can we therefore ascribe to him a unique psychic structure of experience not shared by other human beings? The problem is not the uniqueness of this structure, for Cobb has already argued that humanity has possessed a wealth of such psychic structures in the course of history.[43] If there are a great many differing types, all of which are authentically *human* ways of experience, Jesus could possess a unique type and still be fully human. The problem is rather epistemological: how could we possibly *know* the inner psychic experience of another to ascertain uniquely differing features of his structure? By an analysis of our own structure of experience we can ascertain its common, generic features, and by the analysis of a large class of human beings perhaps we can postulate the particular features of that group's psychic structure, but the inner structure of an individual, particularly when it is claimed to be uniquely different from any other, seems beyond our powers. If we cannot know but only believe, then the question becomes whether we can have any confidence that our belief in such a unique psychic structure is even meaningful.

All of these christological proposals with process theology are strongly influenced by the classical problem, how the Christ can be both fully divine and fully human. But as we have seen, this is no longer the central problem within a Whiteheadian framework. Nor was it the central basis upon which the proclamation of the early church was founded. The basis for the early church was the resurrection. Thus Luke records Peter's speech at Pentecost: "This Jesus God raised up, and of that we all are witnesses. . . .Let all the house of Israel therefore know assuredly that God has made him both Lord and Christ, this Jesus whom you crucified" (Acts 2:32, 36). The classic problem of the status of the Christ came much later. The initial question, which is also the more central question within process Christology, centers on what basis we proclaim Jesus to be the Christ. Our own christological proposal shall follow the lead of the early church, and finds its basis also in the resurrection of Jesus.

NOTES

1. *IL,* p. 112.
2. See *ibid.,* Appendix C, "Objects and Events," pp. 456–69, which explores Thornton's appropriation of Whitehead's categories.

3. *RM*, pp. 110–11; Thornton quotes this sentence, *IL*, p. 463.

4. *SMW*, pp. 156–57; *IL*, p. 460.

5. *IL*, p. 84.

6. To be sure, he assigns them "an altogether different kind of permanence" (*IL*, p. 459) from that of enduring objects, but this difference is left unexplained.

7. *IL*, p. 396:

But if the Trinity be understood in a purely economic sense, so that the distinctions correspond only to aspects of God manifested in His activities of creation, revelation, inspiration or the like, then there are no eternal relations of self-giving within the divine life of Absolute Actuality. Thus the principle of self-giving in God, which is acknowledged to be essential, can find expression only *ad extra*, in relations with creation. But this is to make creation necessary to God, in the sense that the full actuality of God's life is incomplete apart from creation. This is to place God under a necessity *external to Himself*. God becomes dependent upon creation for the expression of His nature.

This is meant to be a *reductio ad absurdum*, but the absurdity is self-imagined. One can almost feel Thornton's horror at the possibility that any aspect of God might be contingent upon the world.

8. *Ibid.*, p. 417:

The created universe is the product of the twofold creative activity of the Word and the Spirit. The Word is the eternal object [= Whitehead's realm of eternal objects as internally ordered] of the Father's self-expression, and the Spirit is the immanent principle of actuality and unity in their mutual relations. So we discern in the organic series a transcendent formative activity of creation weaving patterns of objects upon events, and an immanent energising activity underlying events, and binding their succession into the unity of series and process upon which enduring objects may be patterned.

9. *Ibid.*, pp. 158–59:

With man we stand at the summit of the ascending series, where the progression of the universe and of its modes of revelation and mediation can apparently advance no further.

10. *Ibid.*, p. 223.

11. *Ibid.*, p. 228.

12. *Ibid.*, p. 225.

13. *Ibid.*, p. 227.

14. Norman Pittenger, *The Word Incarnate* (New York: Harper and Brothers, 1959), pp. 107–9. By insisting that Christ enters the series from beyond, "he denies the significance of the whole series as the vehicle of God's action. For in fact the world is *not* patient of deity in any real sense, if at the crucial point it is required that God thus break into his own ordering of things" (p. 108).

15. Charles E. Raven, *Natural Religion and Christian Theology*, vol. 2 (Cambridge: Cambridge University Press, 1953), p. 102: "Dr. Thornton's own doctrine was rendered inconsistent by his insistence that although the creative process disclosed a series of emergents, life, mind, spirit, and thereby foreshadowed the culmination of the series in the coming of Christ, yet that event differed radically from all its predecessors and signalized not the consummation of the process but the intrusion into it of a Being wholly distinct and independent."

16. Dorothy Emmet, *Whitehead's Philosophy of Organism* (London: Macmillan, 1st ed. 1932, 2d ed. 1966), p. 254, n. 2:

He can indeed claim Whitehead's support for the view that our apprehension of the eternal order depends upon the fact of a developing incorporation of that order into the successions of events in Space-Time through an ascending cosmic series [*IL*, p. 98]. But this has really no bearing on the Christology of the latter half of the book, since he claims that Christ is not a product of the creative organic series but an irruption of the Logos-Creator (or the absolute eternal order) into the series.

17. *IL*, pp. 237–38.

18. See the criticism of D. M. Baillie, *God Was in Christ* (New York: Scribner's, 1948), pp. 91–93, who suggests that *The Incarnate Lord* might be understood as a modern version of "the impersonal humanity of Christ" proposed by Cyril of Alexandria. Baillie refers us to a similar critique by J. K. Mozley, *The Doctrine of the Incarnation* (London: G. Bles, 1949), pp. 146–47.

19. J. E. Barnhart, "Incarnation and Process Philosophy," *Religious Studies* 2 (1967), 225–32.

20. *Ibid.*, p. 229. Italics his.

21. *Ibid.*

22. *Ibid.*, p. 231.

23. *RM*, p. 151.

24. *AI*, pp. 214, 216; cf. pp. 166–67.

25. *Ibid.*, p. 216.

26. *Ibid.*, pp. 216, 217.

27. For an extensive bibliography on process Christology, see Ewert H. Cousins, ed., *Process Theology: Basic Writings* (New York: Newman Press, 1971), pp. 200–2, 215–16, and 226. See also Delwin Brown's bibliographic discussion in *Process Philosophy and Christian Thought,* ed. Delwin Brown, Ralph E. James, Jr., and Gene Reeves (Indianapolis: Bobbs-Merrill, 1971), pp. 58–61. I have specifically criticized Ronald L. Williams's article as paradigmatic of this approach in "The Possibilities for Process Christology," *Encounter* 35/4 (Autumn 1974), 281–94, esp. pp. 283–86. For my additional comments on Griffin's *A Process Christology*, see pp. 286–94.

28. *PC*, p. 218.

29. *Ibid.*, p. 220; italics his.

30. *Ibid.*, p. 218. Here God's eternal character and purpose refer to his personal attributes which can to some extent be embodied by a finite being sharing the same character and purpose, in contradistinction to God's metaphysical attributes, which indicate his uniqueness from all finite beings (*PC*, pp. 191–92). Nevertheless, both are aspects of God's uncreated abstract essence. Griffin does not avail himself of the distinction proposed by Pailin, whereby God's personal attributes are those values which God has in fact chosen for all occasions in this actual world. In either case, however, such personal attributes would be knowable in the same way that his metaphysical attributes are, namely, by way of philosophical inquiry. See David A. Pailin, "The Incarnation as a Continuing Reality," *Religious Studies* 6/4 (December 1970), 303–27, and my response, "The Incarnation as a Contingent Reality," *Religious Studies* 8/2 (June 1972), 169–73.

31. *PC*, p. 220.

32. I. S. Shklovskii and Carl Sagan, *Intelligent Life in the Universe* (San Francisco: Holden-Day, 1966), p. 166.

33. Paul Tillich, *Systematic Theology,* vol. 2 (Chicago: The University of Chicago Press, 1957), p. 95.

34. Individual cells within a complex organism, to be sure, apparently have a shorter life-span than their host. It may be, however, that the kind of organization whereby the individual cells are knit together is itself simpler than the organization of the cell. Bureaucracies and institutions are less organically structured than individual human beings, yet they can outlast a score of human life-spans. If survival, that is, that persistence of a given state of organization, is our sole criterion of value, then there is a lot to be said for institutional inertia. It is highly adaptive in its ability to survive most anything.

35. Sir Alister Hardy, *The Living Stream: Evolution and Man* (London: William Collins, 1965).

36. The argument of this paragraph is heavily dependent upon Richard H. Overman, *Evolution and the Christian Doctrine of Creation* (Philadelphia: Westminster Press, 1967), pp. 203–11.

37. Erwin Schrodinger, *Mind and Matter* (Cambridge University press, 1959), pp. 4–5.

38. Tillich, *Systematic Theology,* vol. 2, p. 96.

39. Cobb's theory of incarnation is complex, and perhaps best understood by considering it in a simpler version, as presented in chapter 6 of *Process Theology, An Introductory Exposition,* by John B. Cobb, Jr., and David Ray Griffin (Philadelphia: Westminster Press, 1976). There Christ signifies not only Jesus but *any* incarnation of the Word or Logos of God. Since the Logos is identified with God's primordial nature, that is, with the totality of the possibilities God envisages for the world, Christ, its incarnation, is seen in the actualization of any radically new and creative possibilities derived from God. Hence we can see that such actualization must result in creative transformation. This theme of Christ as creative transformation is emphasized in *Christ in a Pluralistic Age,* but it is overlaid by *another* account of Christ, namely, as the particularization of divine aims in images or symbols capable of evoking deep human response. There are thus two layers of meaning as to Christ in this work, neither of which allows for the conventional simple identification of Christ with Jesus only.

40. Cobb acknowledges his indebtedness for the idea to William Beardslee, *A House for Hope* (Philadelphia: Westminster Press, 1972): see *CPA,* pp. 14–15.

Beardslee reports that the thesis of Donald W. Sherburne's *A Whiteheadian Aesthetic* (New Haven: Yale University Press, 1961), that a work of art has the ontological status of a Whiteheadian proposition, suggested the idea to him.

41. Whitehead quotes these words from the frontispiece of Cardinal Newman's *Grammar of Assent, AI* 380: *"Non in dialectica complacuit Deo salvum facere populum suum."*

42. John Cobb, Jr., "A Whiteheadian Christology," in *Process Philosophy and Christian Thought,* pp. 382–98.

43. John Cobb, Jr., *The Structure of Christian Existence* (Philadelphia: Westminster Press, 1967) describes eight types for human existence. Now Cobb sees these types as ranged along a continuum.

CHAPTER 5

The Resurrection as the Emergence of the Body of Christ

In responding to the New Testament witness to the resurrection, much depends upon the interpretative categories we select to evaluate that testimony. Wolfhart Pannenberg urges us to adopt, in its essential outline, the anticipation of a general resurrection from the dead as the only adequate context within which to judge the evidence. "Only the traditional expectation of the end of history rooted in apocalyptic gave Paul the opportunity of designating the particular event that he experienced, as Jesus' other disciples had experienced it previously, as an event belonging to the category of resurrection life. There, Paul called the expectation of a resurrection of the dead the presupposition for the recognition of Jesus' resurrection: 'If the dead are not raised, then Christ has not been raised' (1 Cor. 15:16)."[1]

Commenting on this same text, Gordon D. Kaufman remarks: "If, now, we bring a different framework of interpretation from Jewish apocalypticism to this critical event in which Christian faith was born—as we must—we should not be overly surprised or dismayed when we find it necessary to understand the character of the event somewhat differently from the first Christians."[2] He goes on to argue that the resurrection appearances were essentially hallucinations that the disciples mistakenly interpreted as Jesus come back from the dead, but that God used these hallucinations and this misinterpretation to create his kingdom, his community of love and forgiveness, within human history. I agree with Kaufman that the emergence of this community embodies the reality of the resurrection here on earth, and that the apocalyptic expectation must be discarded. I disagree with him, however, on the one point where he makes common cause with Pannenberg: namely, that apart from the apocalyptic horizon, the disciples' experiences can only be regarded as subjective hallucinations.

Consider, for the moment, Isaiah's experience in the temple in the year that King Uzziah died. He reports, "I saw the Lord sitting upon a throne, high and lifted up; and his train filled the temple" (Isa. 6:1). Was this an hallucination? On the one hand, there are elements I take to be primarily subjective in Isaiah's experience—the bodily figure seated on the throne. On the other hand, I do not doubt Isaiah's claim that he "saw" the Lord, that is, that he actually encountered the divine reality distinct from himself in a particularly vivid manner. I would not call this experience an hallucination, which I take to be purely subjective in all important respects, having no significant objective referent, but rather a vision, the encounter with a nonperceptual reality made manifest and perceptible by hallucinatory means. Thus a vision stands halfway between an hallucination and veridical experience, and is needed in this case because neither of these alternatives adequately accounts for Isaiah's experience. To be sure, my judgment is dependent upon the interpretive framework I have adopted, which assumes that God is real independently of the believer and that God cannot be sensuously perceived. If we reject the first assumption, Isaiah's experience can only be hallucinatory; if, on the other hand, we reject only the second, then his experience might be taken as completely veridical.

We take 1 Corinthians 15 to be our most reliable testimony to the resurrection appearances, as being the only eyewitness report we have. Was Paul's experience on the road to Damascus a vision or an hallucination? We rule out the third possibility of veridical experience on the testimony of Luke in Acts, who reports a light from heaven and a voice, which we take to be hallucinatory accompaniments. Paul speaks of a "spiritual body" later on in that chapter, and it may well be that he took the Christ he encountered to be embodied in a perceptible spiritual body, but if so, it is remarkable that he never attempts to distinguish this spiritual body belonging solely to the resurrected Christ from the body of Christ which is the church. At any rate, we take the risen Christ to be living but not perceptible, and so the means whereby Christ became audible and (perhaps) visible to Paul were essentially hallucinatory. What we need at this point is an interpretive framework permitting us so to specify the possibility of the objective reality of the risen Christ that

Paul's experience may be approached as a vision rather than as an hallucination. Pannenberg claims that this can only be found in the apocalyptic expectation of a general resurrection, but I wish to propose an alternative to accomplish the same purpose.

Before proceeding to this task, however, let us pause to note that if the risen Christ is essentially nonperceptible, we should not expect testimony to certain appearances to be our primary witness to his resurrection. I take this to be the case. The earliest Christians did not believe in the resurrection primarily because they accepted the apostles' reports, but because they experienced the Spirit of Christ alive and active in their midst. As John Knox argues, "The two facts—he was known still and he was remembered—constitute together the miracle of the Resurrection; and neither is more important than the other."[3] This nonperceptual yet real experience of Christ's directing activity in and through their lives assured the early believers that he was alive. Since they also remembered that he had died, they could only infer that he must have risen from the dead. The resurrection appearances confirmed this conviction, to be sure, but these visions may have been originally understood as grants of apostolic authority to their recipients, as fuller manifestations of the risen Christ bestowed upon the privileged few chosen to be their leaders. Only when the sense of the immediate presence of Christ in their midst faded would these reports be reconceived primarily as testimony to the resurrection. Yet, as with the resurrection appearances, such nonperceptual experiences of the living Christ also depend upon an interpretive framework, one which permits the presence of the living Christ to be a real possibility for the believer. For if this possibility is excluded on *a priori* grounds, the experience must be interpreted another way: as an unwarranted enthusiasm, as the presence of human love in community, as the activity of God mediated through the community's memory of Jesus, or what have you.

As a clue to an alternative interpretive framework, I wish to suggest a different way of understanding the "spiritual body," one which Paul may have been groping for but was prevented from reaching by his preconceptions about the general resurrection. Usually this is taken to mean a body which is no longer "corporeal" or material but composed rather of some more ethereal substance. The adjective "spiritual" then signifies the material cause of that body, to use Aristotelian language. In contrast I understand the adjective to refer to that which permeates, vivifies, and directs the body for its own purposes. Here it is important to note that the contrasting term, "physical body" (RSV), is not *soma phusikon* but *soma psuchikon,* a "psychical body." This does not mean that ordinary human body is composed of some psychical material, but that this physical body is animated by a soul or mind or psyche which organizes and directs its activity. The New English Bible translation is to be preferred: "If there is such a thing as an animal body [cf. Vulgate: *corpus animale*], there is also a spiritual body" (1 Cor. 15:44). Or perhaps we should say, the human body is animate because of the presence of the *anima* or soul. Thus Paul continues: "It is in this sense that Scripture says, 'The first man, Adam, became an animate being,' whereas the last Adam has become a life-giving spirit" (1 Cor. 15:45 NEB). The actions of the spiritual body are animated and directed by that life-giving spirit of the last Adam, that man who stands on the threshold of a new emergent reality, the body of Christ. This body here and now is composed of many human members, of flesh and blood, but it is a spiritual body because it is animated by the spirit of Christ.

This transformed human community forms a living organism, a biological phenomenon which we conceive to be the next stage in the emergent evolution of the world, and the incarnation of the divine Word. As long as we think of this Word as the expression of God's underlying character or eternal purpose, we overlook its contingent relatedness to the evolving world. It does express God's creative character and his fundamental purpose in bringing the world into fullness of being, but that is only its abstract essence. The creative Word embodies God's general power of the future acting on all creatures, but the concrete character of the creative Word must be found in the specific way in which it addresses each species to evolve beyond itself. If by the Christ-event we mean the human actualization of this creative Word, we must bear in mind the contingent aspects of God's address to man, for this address must be so coordinated with the human situation as to provide the means for a new creation transforming man. God's purpose in Christ is not merely to manifest his love to all mankind (though it intends that as well), but to establish a new organic unity transcending human fragmentariness. Such action requires a means growing out of our particular conditions and opportunities. That purpose in Christ embodies God's general aim for all creation in the specific way appropriate to man, and both foci must be considered in any full account.

God has purposes for us in every moment of our existence, some rather trivial, others quite profound. His underlying aim is always the same, for he seeks our welfare both for our sakes and as the condition for his own welfare. This basic aim, however, is expressed in specific purposes appropriate to the particular conditions and opportunities confronting us at particular times. We may respond wholly or partially to these particular purposes by actualizing them in concrete fact; to that extent God's purposes become incarnate in the world. As we have seen, some argue that the Christ was the incarnation of the Word of God because he fully realized the divine purpose. While this may well be necessary, it is not a sufficient condition to designate the particular character of the Christ. This is not adequate grounds for distinguishing between Jesus and Socrates and Gautama, let alone any number of other wise or saintly or good people, unless one resorts to a dogmatic insistence upon Jesus' "sinlessness" or "absolute perfection" about which we have no final way of knowing, and which Jesus is reported as denying with respect to himself (Mark 10:18). Not all divine aims are (or could be) christological aims, for it is only under very special circumstances within human life that God could introduce, as relevant to those conditions and opportunities, that aim capable of transforming man beyond himself. We define this christological aim—God's purpose in Christ—to be the creative emergence of a new organic unity incorporating man, and confess that this aim was realized in the life, death, and resurrection of Jesus of Nazareth.

Both the granting of this christological aim and its receptive realization required prior preparation. To be relevant and usefully significant, God's particular purpose must be realizable under the existent conditions. Sometimes these conditions only permit meager results. In other circumstances the concrete realization of God's preliminary aims may create the conditions for a further intensification of divine aim. We may see in the life of Israel and in the personal life of Jesus just such an intensification, creating the conditions such that God's culminating aims for man could become relevant for realization. God calls every man, but some like Abraham respond more fully to that call. In the light of the patriarch's wandering with God in the land of Canaan, Moses could be called to lead the children of Israel into the promised land. Because of Israel's covenant with God in the wilderness, the prophets could call upon the people to return to that covenant, proclaiming to them the divine intent in their historical situation. Through this process Israel could become a special locus of God's creative purposes for mankind, purposes it might realize or bequeath to another to realize. God has no fixed, inalterable plan here, but everywhere seeks inexorably to urge creation beyond itself. We may interpret the biblical record as God seeking to further this aim first with all mankind, then with his chosen people Israel, then with the faithful remnant, finally with that individual person willing to embody in his own life the meaning, hopes, and mission God has entrusted to Israel.

In order to see the particular character of the divine aim actualized in the Christ-event, we may speculate a bit upon the evolutionary advance of the world by considering its possible future development. Heretofore, this earth has witnessed the emergence of single-celled living organisms, the growth of multicelled plant organisms, the advent of animals with centralized nervous systems making self-directed activity possible, and the flowering of humanity with its far-flung culture. In this evolutionary process we may discern an unfolding spiral development whereby later phases recapitulate earlier ones on a higher level. Thus animals for the most part have little or no social organization, and in this respect may be likened to single-celled organisms. With the emergence of symbolic communication permitting the transmission of cultural traditions from generation to generation, man has been able to develop a highly complex social life allowing for a high degree of specialization and interdependence among its members. Such human social organization may be compared with the life of plants, whose individual cells may be highly specialized and interdependent. In both cases the focus of life remains on the individual level, for there is no coordinating agency directing the life of the plant or the activities of an ordinary human society as a whole. A tree is a democracy of cells, Whitehead wrote. In both cases individual members may exercise some dominance over others, in particular by altering the patterns guiding further growth and development, but the social coordination stems from basic patterns embodied in the genetic makeup of the plant cells and in the laws and traditions of human culture. Mankind has grown together into ever more involuted social patterns dead-ending in the unfeeling excesses of bureaucracy, and longs for liberation from this kind of bondage to the law. The law killeth, for these social traditions which made human community possible are increasingly restrictive of human initiative along novel lines, affording maximum freedom only to those content to develop along established patterns.

Some humans romantically yearn for a regression back to social anarchy, which might be likened—rather fancifully, to be sure—to the cells of a plant longing for the mobility of single-celled organisms. A more viable option may lie in the emergence of dynamic human societies more nearly analogous to animals possessing minds coordinating the activities of the body. It is not essential to bodies that their individual components be spatially contiguous if we see that the basic relationship involved connects an active coordinating agency with the subordinate instrumentality providing it with expression. The eleventh-century Hindu theologian Ramanuja defined a body as any substance or actuality "which a sentient soul is capable of controlling and supporting for its own purposes, and which stands to that soul in an entirely subordinate relation."[4] We adopt this broad definition, which does not entail spatial contiguity. Plant and animal cells must be spatially contiguous in order to permit the interchange of material necessary to sustain life, but mankind has been able to organize commerce and economic interdependence by other means. The transformation of human society, or some part of it, into a living body does not require greater proximity or necessarily more complex organization—we're crowded enough as it is. More importantly, it awaits the emergence of a dynamic, responsive agency capable of coordinating the activities of a human society as a whole, within which human individuals might find themselves to be the willing, freely responsive instrumentalities of a higher will. This the early church found in the risen Christ, whom to serve is perfect freedom. Now, Paul exults, life in the Spirit sets us free from the necessity of the law.[5]

Within the body of Christ the early Christians experienced God's Spirit, the presence of divine purposing in their lives to which they could respond. They also experienced the Spirit of Christ as a living agency providing aims and directions for their corporate existence. The Spirit of Christ must have had its own distinctive personality, for they recognized that it bore unmistakable continuity with their master Jesus whom they remembered. Paul's letters show the difficulty they had in relating the Spirit of Christ to the Spirit of God, since the aims they received from Christ were first derived from God. As the directing mind of his body, the risen Christ serves as the channel for the intensification of divine aims. The cells in my index finger are quite limited in terms of what they may achieve on their own, for their individual activity is restricted to processes of growth, oxygen exchange, homeostatic adjustment, and the like. Their individual capacity to serve God's purposes is rather small. These same cells as part of my hand, however, can serve as instrumentalities accomplishing the aims of my mind, such as the typing of this chapter. Likewise as members of the body of Christ, humans may be achieving aims which far transcend human imagination. God can work through us directly by means of his aims actualized by us individually, but much more powerfully through the mediating agency of Christ.

According to the tradition reported by Paul and the Gospel writers, Peter encountered Jesus as Lord and Christ on the third day after his death. In what form Christ appeared to Peter we do not know; nor is it important, for we regard it as an hallucinatory accompaniment to the actual encounter. Peter experienced the Spirit of Christ, a nonperceptible reality proposing aims for guiding the actions of Peter directly analogous to the nonperceptible reality of the human mind as guiding the actions of the body. Peter encountered a Spirit he knew to be one with the extraordinary life of the Master he had followed, a Spirit to whom he could now fully dedicate himself in the confidence that the aims and directives it mediated served God's purposes, just as Jesus had served those purposes during his lifetime. Moreover, this Spirit was living, dynamic, responsive to growing circumstance. As others encountered this same reality, they too became the instrumentalities of its will, as they became knit together into that common life we know as the body of Christ. Peter and the others experienced this dynamic presence in their midst as shaping their common activities; they remembered Jesus' life and death and could interpret this phenomenon in only one way, proclaimed by Peter at Pentecost: This Jesus, whom you crucified, God has raised up and made both Lord and Christ (Acts 2:23–24, 36).

We argue for the bodily resurrection of Christ, but the body of Christ's resurrection is none other than the body of Christ which is the church, understood as that emergent community of love guided by the dynamic activity of Christ's Spirit. According to Luke and Paul, Simon Peter was the first person to form that body whose mind is the risen Christ, thereby effecting the bodily resurrection. If the critics are correct in associating

Peter's confession, placed by Mark at Caesarea Philippi, with this resurrection encounter, we may be permitted an additional insight into the appended saying recorded by Matthew (16:17–19). As the first member of the body of Christ, Peter is the rock or foundation for the building up of the church, the cell to which all other cells are attached in the growth of that body.

This resurrection is thus the incarnation of the divine Word addressed to the human situation. The incarnation is not located solely or even primarily in the life of Jesus, although without that life it could not have occurred then. The incarnation was the total event of the emergence of the body of Christ. It required a human life totally open to divine purposing, a life others could completely trust as from God. Yet it also requires the emergence of a new community knit together by the power of God. Initially the continued identity of Jesus was objectively sustained in the memory of his disciples. As these disciples responded to the desires and aims of God as concentrated through this memory by the interpenetration of their concerns for one another in love, the organic life they knit together was able to support the renewed subjectivity of the risen Christ, in the same way a living body can support a living mind.

In Christ we become a new creation; old things have passed away. It began with the human life of Jesus, but culminates in his being "raised up," both as the living Head of the body and as "seated in heavenly place" at the right hand of God, thus becoming a privileged means of interaction and mediation between God and man.

For this process Christology, then, the resurrection of Jesus is hardly an optional belief.[6] It is its very heart. It forms the basis of our understanding of what God effected in the Christ-event.

NOTES

1. Wolfhart Pannenberg, *Jesus—God and Man* (Philadelphia: Westminster Press, 1969), p. 81.

2. Gordon D. Kaufman, *Systematic Theology: A Historicist Perspective* (New York: Scribner's, 1968), p. 422, n. 22.

3. John Knox, *The Early Church and the Coming Great Church* (Nashville: Abingdon Press, 1955), pp. 52–53.

4. As quoted by James S. Helfer in "The Body of Brahman According to Ramanuja," *Journal of Bible and Religion* 32 (1964), 44.

5. Although there are obvious affinities between my reasoning and the thought of Teilhard de Chardin, his discussion of the body of Christ focuses rather upon the indi-

vidual Christian's incorporation within Christ as the Omega point toward which all creation moves. Teilhard makes reference to the Pauline texts concerning the body of Christ,
but he is primarily intent upon showing how the Christian is related to Christ's cosmic role
as the hope of all creation. See Christopher F. Mooney, *Teilhard de Chardin and the
Mystery of Christ* (New York: Harper & Row, 1966), pp. 83–103, esp. pp. 87–94.
Mooney provides a useful summary of Paul's teaching concerning the body of Christ
which comes very close to my interpretation, were it not for the unwarranted introduction
of the notion of the "Body-Person of Christ" (pp. 94, 100).

Unlike Teilhard's, my analysis does not require us to accord mankind some privileged
centrality in God's creative design. The body of Christ need not be the final culmination of
the creative process. It is rather the next stage in the evolutionary advance on the planet
Earth, of overwhelming importance to us humans at this time, but perhaps only one
among myriads given God's creative activity on other worlds. The resurrected Christ is
the incarnation of the Word of God, but only of that Word as specifically addressed to the
particular situation of mankind.

6. *PC*, p. 12. Clark Williamson challenges Griffin's claim in his review, *Process
Studies* 4/3 (Fall 1974), 212–17.

CHAPTER 6

Reconciliation through the Cross

God was in Christ as the divine address for man actualized in the life, death, and resurrection of Jesus. He was also in Christ inasmuch as Jesus' personal existence revealed the divine perspective upon mankind, for he encountered and experienced our predicament with all the patience, the care, and the longing for our well-being that God bestows upon us. In the last chapter we saw how in Christ's resurrection we can be raised to newness of life, exchanging our separate, self-justifying individual existences for corporate participation in the body of Christ, whose manifold cells are coordinated and directed by the living purposes of its transhuman psyche, the risen Christ. Now we need to consider how this resurrection was prepared for by the suffering and death of Jesus. It not only made the original event possible, but it continues to make our own incorporation within this body possible by the reconciling work of God effected in Christ.

In the final high-priestly prayer, John records these words for Jesus: "I glorified thee on earth, having accomplished the work which thou gavest me to do; and now, Father, glorify thou me in thine own presence with the glory which I had with thee before the world was made" (John 17:4–5). These words are spoken in anticipation of the cross, when all would be accomplished, and express John's assumption of a subjective preexistence of Christ, for his exalted state in resurrection is understood as a restoration of his former glory. Our attention is drawn to the twofold act of glorification depicted here: God glorifies Christ in resurrection, while he glorifies God in crucifixion. Exaltation to the right hand of power is certainly glorification. The crucifixion is no less glorification, if it is understood primarily in terms of revelation. The Old Testament spoke of the *Shekhinah*, the glorious visible manifestation of the invisible God, for no manifestation of God's presence among us could be less than glorious. The shocking reversal of the gospel, underscored by John, is that God is most decisively glorified to us in this execution of a criminal and blasphemer.

John Courtney Murray has said that while the Old Testament speaks to us of God, only the New Testament reveals this same God to be the God and Father of our Lord Jesus Christ.[1] In his teaching and healing ministry Jesus certainly acted out an intimacy with his heavenly Father that startled contemporary Jewish piety, but his deepest revelation of God's profound empathy for us was reserved for the agony of the cross. This dimension of God's being, however, though hinted at in tentative probings in the Old Testament literature,[2] was indignantly suppressed in classical theism by Greek ideals of perfection, which dictated absolute impassibility to God. To safeguard this divine impassibility, it even decreed two natures in Christ, one divine and one human, holding that in his crucifixion he suffered as man, but not as God. Our teaching is precisely the opposite: in no event did Jesus more fully demonstrate the love of God than in his passion! In this God was truly glorified.

Classical theism, despite its insistence upon the divinity of Christ, wishes to make the crucifixion into a purely human act. But this would have no saving significance for us. The resurrection is the presupposition of the cross, as Jürgen Moltmann has recently reminded us.[3] Without the resurrection, Jesus' execution is no different from the crucifixion of countless Christian martyrs after him, or the stoning of the prophets before him. He would have died as one of the heroes of the faith, along with the saints and martyrs, inspiring us by his fearless example and profound teaching, but not saving us from our sins and reconciling us to God. Who can forgive us for our sins, save God alone? If God works through Jesus to reconcile us to himself, this must embrace the suffering this entails. If this is the cross of the Risen One, then the vindication of Jesus as the supreme revelation of God certainly includes the depths of this suffering.

Whitehead's original conception of God as the principle of limitation in *Science and the Modern World,* like classical theism, had no room for divine passivity. Subsequently he enlarged this with an appreciation of God's consequent or receptive nature. With Whitehead we can make a formal distinction between two natures or aspects of God's actuality: his primordial nature as the locus of all pure possibilities, which God draws upon in order to provide the initial aims for each emerging event, and his consequent nature as the ultimate recipient of all actuality, which is perfectly experienced and treasured within God. Naturally these two aspects of God reciprocally influence each other: God's provision of initial aims is particularized and made relevant to the world in terms of his consequent experience, and the way God treasures this experience draws heavily upon the infinite resources of his primordial imagination. While a full account of the divine dynamics must perforce dwell on these interactions, we may briefly consider these distinct natures by an abstraction of reason.

We may equally well designate the primordial aspect the nontemporal dimension of God's being, for it is God conceived of as divorced from time, wholly independent of the world, timelessly envisioning the entire multiplicity of pure possibilities. It is Aristotle's God "thinking on thinking." Alternatively, it is the God of the Old Testament in his role as creator, lawmaker, and judge. To be sure, Whitehead does not conceive of God as the efficient maker of the universe, fashioning it out of nothing. Rather, his God conforms to the image of the Priestly writers in Genesis 1, who commands the world to be. This realm of pure possibility forms the Word by which God commands and creates. This same realm provides all the pure forms of value, in terms of which each effort of the finite world is evoked, and in terms of which its final achievement is judged. This lure of God entices the creative advance onward, and simultaneously serves as the ideal standard by which its results are measured.

The passive, receptive aspect of God's being is consequent upon the ongoing activity of the temporal world. It is, we may say, God's temporal nature. In himself, God is independent of time, but temporal succession is a fundamental reality of the world, the chief means whereby it can support a vast multiplicity of finite, exclusive actualities. Three solutions have been offered as to how a nontemporal God could be related to a temporal world. (1) God and the world are radically distinct, at least from the divine perspective, and so God is ignorant of this dull, sublunary world (Aristotle). (2) God knows the world, but because his knowledge is nontemporal yet penetrates to the reality of things, the temporality of the world is finally merely apparent. This is the upshot of classical theism, and the basic implication of God's knowledge of future contingents. There seems to be no way a purely nontemporal God can know a temporal world without violating that world's temporal integrity. (3) God's eternal nature is supplemented by a temporal nature, itself directly dependent upon the world's finite actualizations for its concrete content of experience. In himself God knows only pure, unbroken, nontemporal unity, but this knowledge is further enriched by the temporal experience of the world's plurality. This consequent knowledge is cumulative and temporal, following the contours of the world's unfolding reality.

The thoroughgoing coherence of Whitehead's philosophy demands these two natures in God. God is an actuality, even the chief exemplification of the category of actual entities,[4] and all actualities have both conceptual and physical prehensions. Without these additional physical prehensions, God would have no experience of the world, whose plurality and finitude require temporality. On the other hand, the experiential evidence for the divine consequent nature is very subtle and tenuous. For this reason Whitehead postpones its introduction as long as possible in his two major metaphysical works. In *Process and Reality,* the consequent nature is considered only in the last eleven pages,[5] while its counterpart, "an Adventure in the Universe as One," is mentioned only on the last two pages of *Adventures of Ideas.*[6] The structure of both works is the same: for the most part Whitehead is content to justify his doctrines by an appeal to average, ordinary experience, although experience is understood more richly than its analysis in classical empiricism would indicate. In this one instance, however, he warns us that "any cogency of argument entirely depends upon elucidation of somewhat exceptional elements in our conscious experience—those elements which may roughly be classed together as religious and moral intuitions."[7]

These words should not be misunderstood as a traditional appeal to revelation. At least two factors militate against such an interpretation. In the first place, Whitehead takes an evolutionary view of experience, reminding us that our ordinary, waking consciousness was once highly extraordinary among our primate ancestors. Thus it is quite conceivable that in the future the extraordinary deliverances of religious and moral intuitions will appear quite ordinary. Secondly, Whitehead is at all times interested in discerning the generic, invariant structures of experience, not their contingent contents. Insofar as revelation diverges from reason, it does so in terms of such contingent content. Revelation has sought to apprise us of the favored role of Israel or of the divine significance of the life and death of Jesus of Nazareth, contingencies which in the nature of things philosophic generalization knows not of. If revelation has sought to teach us of the mysteries of the Trinity transcending human reason, we must remember that its reflection began in the effort to understand just how God and the person of Jesus are to be related, and must make allowance for the partial or total eclipse of specific revelational content by the overlay of philosophical speculation. Inasmuch as Whitehead always seeks for philosophically generic features, disregarding specific historical particulars, we must suppose that the impress of the consequent nature is a pervasive feature of all experience, yet unnoticed except in all but the most sensitive religious experiences.

The initial aim guiding each act of becoming to fruition is a pervasive feature of all actuality, yet only humankind, to our knowledge, is con-sciously aware of it. Our perception of the initial aims provided by God is a measure of our moral sensitivity. Frequently, however, these moral norms are taken to be absolute and invariant, regardless of circumstance. No flexibility or sensitivity to changing situations is permitted. This would be the case if the initial aims provided by the primordial nature were not tempered and modulated in any way by God's consequent ex-perience. In that case, however, moral norms would either be too general to be relevant and useful, or so specific as to be unduly restrictive.

If this were the only side of his character, the primordial nature of a personal God could easily become the impersonal standard of values such as Plato's Form of the Good. With the consequent nature, however, God is unmistakably personal. We do not directly apprehend his consequent nature, but become aware of its presence by the subtle, dynamic shifts in the divine aims directly accessible to us as God responds to our actions. This is the meaning of a very enigmatic statement that appears on the very last page of *Process and Reality*: "Throughout the perishing occasions in the life of each temporal Creature, the inward source of distaste or of refreshment, the judge arising out of the very nature of things, redeemer or goddess of mischief, is the transformation of Itself, everlasting in the Being of God."[8] This inward source of distaste or of refreshment is the series of initial aims received from God, which both judge our previous achievements, and give us courage to strive anew. If the best be bad, it appears under the guise of the goddess of mischief, providing only the best possibility for that impasse.[9] Yet it can also redeem. The individual, momentary occasions of our life, with their particular, limited accomplishments, pass away, yet not before they are caught up and transformed in the divine life, informing and qualifying those initial aims which God then supplies our successive occasions. These new aims are not impervious to our past, but express God's living response and encouragement to our faltering actions.

In the biblical imperative "You must be born *anew*" (John 3:3), the same Greek word *anōthen* may also mean: "from above." Both meanings of this rich ambiguity are relevant to our argument. In terms of the perishing occasions of our temporal life, we are being born anew and from above as we receive novel initial aims from God originating our subjectivity from moment to moment. It is possible for us to be blind to this inward source, insisting upon the solid, substantial endurance of our old selfhood, but the experience of reconciliation in nearness to God calls forth the newness of life that this interior dialogue evokes. It is God's consequent experience of our lives which calls forth his dynamic provision of new aims for our lives, by which we have redemption.

Ancient Israel was never tempted to replace the lawgiver with the law, following Plato's example. It had a lively sense of God's personal involvement in the history of his people. To that extent its teachings clearly anticipate what Whitehead designates as the temporal or consequent nature of God. Yet combined with the image of God as the righteous judge, this divine responsiveness quickly issued into the threat of rejection in the face of Israel's sinfulness. The New Testament proclaims that no matter how evil the sin, God stands ready to receive the sinner and to forgive the sin. He stands ready to receive into his own being all the evil of the world to bring about its transformation, and this experience of evil is the divine suffering epitomized by the crucifixion. This is the most profound manifestation of the presence of the consequent nature in our experience.

Yet the dynamics of divine reconciliation is subtle, and it is all too easy for some commentators to emphasize the consequent character of God's activity at the expense of his primordial character. This appears to be the case with the most extensive reflection to date upon the work of Christ within a process context, Don S. Browning's *Atonement and Psychotherapy*.[10] As the title indicates, Browning proposes to understand the atonement in terms of an analogy drawn from Carl Rogers's theory of psychotherapeutic healing. According to this view, the neurotic person cannot rely spontaneously upon his total experiencing process because some of his feelings are inadmissible to his own awareness.[11] He has placed conditions of worth upon himself, conditions by which he can accept his actions, and these same conditions, largely appropriated from his own social matrix, exclude certain elements of his behavior and feeling as unacceptable. The healing process calls for the unconditioned empathic acceptance of the client's feelings by the therapist. He must feel his client's feelings fully, yet empathetically rather than sympathetically. If the therapist were to experience these feelings under the same conditions of worth that the client attaches to them, he would become alarmed and attempt to fend off the same feelings the client was trying to avoid.[12] He must show the client how to accept the full range of his experiencing, and thereby overcome the inner division within his soul.

Browning makes fully clear to us the sinfulness of our bondage to our conditions of worth, but not the sinfulness of our violation of these standards. In the context of his analysis focusing upon the therapeutic relationship, these conditions of worth are uniformly depreciated as that which the good therapist does without as much as possible. In criticizing Anselm's concept of sin as a violation of God's honor, Browning protests that this implies some condition of worth within God. "It would, in effect, place within the Godhead a neurotic element that can never serve as a solid presupposition for the salvation of man."[13] God is completely without conditions of worth qualifying his empathic acceptance, and this unconditionedness constitutes the primary sense in which God is law. "This primary sense in which God is love and law must be kept separate from other ways of referring to God's law. The secondary sense in which God is law refers to the means-end structures of coercion designed to keep the human situation integrated so that his law and love in the primary sense can operate with enhanced effectiveness."[14] In neither sense, then, does divine law sanction moral norms. Unconditioned acceptance transcends such norms, while "the means-end structures of coercion" can only refer to the laws of nature whereby human freedom is kept within constructive bounds.[15]

Perhaps we may distinguish between values functioning as creative goals and values used as conditions of worth. The specific content of these values may be the same, although their use is different. In the first instance, these goals derived from God serve as a focus for creaturely striving; in the second, as a means of exclusion whereby other values are ignored, destroyed, or suppressed. Yet, as Whitehead saw, these two roles are so bound up with one another that some values are inevitably lost. "In the temporal world, it is the empirical fact that process entails loss: the past is present under an abstraction . . . . The nature of evil is that the characters of things are mutually obstructive. Thus the depths of life require a process of selection."[16] Every actualization is a finite achievement cutting off all other possibilities for that particular situation and eliminating all elements received from its immediate inheritance which are incompatible with that one outcome decided upon. In human experience, this elimination may take the form of dismissing the unwanted element into the subconscious mind.

In general, if one takes into account all stages of evolutionary development, the elimination inherent in finite actualization takes two basic forms. In simpler organisms the large bulk of incompatible elements are simply never included in the first place, for the organism is incapable of absorbing and responding to them. Thus the behavior of elementary particles and atoms can be explained solely in terms of physical influences because psychological, cultural, or other such influences have no impact upon them. The more complex organisms, on the other hand, are capable of receiving and responding to more influences derived from their immediate situation than they can handle and therefore must eliminate some of these in the very process of achieving a definite result. Thus a molecule's experience is "unconscious" because it is incapable of raising any of its feelings into consciousness, while the subconscious reaches of our experience have been suppressed in the interests of some definite conscious outcome.

Simpler organisms, including animals, may be largely understood in terms of the Aristotelian concept of entelechy, as spontaneously fulfilling their inherent goals in terms of resources ordinarily commensurate with these goals. In man, however, conscious awareness of goals as moral norms takes precedence, because the freedom consequent upon greatly expanded resources requires more explicit focus. For much of our activity and experience, these moral norms need to function as conditions of worth excluding much of our potential resources for the sake of definite, stable outcomes. These conditions of worth are not bad in themselves, but they can become the barrier to further self-growth if allowed to become rigid, and the allegiance to old values can make us impervious to the emergence of new values.

Unconditioned empathic acceptance means that God has no intrinsic conditions of worth restricting his own experience and activity, but this does not mean that he has no such conditions for his creatures. Here we must distinguish between the diverse roles of God and his creatures. God is infinitely receptive, receiving from his creatures the measure of finite actuality he acquires. The finite and ultimately arbitrary character of temporal actualization prevents us from ascribing it directly to God's own activity. His function is to foster and direct the process of actualization carried on by his creatures, and to redress the inevitable loss involved by integrating all of its results into his living experience. In the first role he is the ultimate source of all our values, which serve both as lures for achievement and as conditions of worth by which our achievements may be judged. In the latter role God is the ultimate preserver of all, embracing both our achievements and failures, thereby overcoming the destruction inherent in finite achievement.

The analogy of the therapist adequately describes God's second, consequent role, but may distort the role of value-commitments both for God and the therapist. We may say that God acts without values in his unconditioned acceptance, but values govern both the initial aims he proposes to his creatures and the way in which what he has fully accepted becomes organized and integrated into his own experience. Likewise the therapist in Browning's eyes may seek to eliminate all value-conditions from the therapeutic relationship, but this very effort is both motivated and judged by the specific aim of healing the client's neuroses.

Browning distinguishes between feelings and behavior, arguing that behavior should be controlled by conditions of worth, but not feelings, all of which are acceptable. But our feelings of failure and worthlessness ordinarily relate to our behavior, which would have no focus or direction apart from these value-conditions. What is needed is not an elimination of value-conditions, but their relativization: the possibility of their expansion and growth, and the possibility that failures relative to these values can somehow be redeemed. The therapist in unconditional acceptance conveys that redemption to the client, but the ultimate basis for such acceptance lies in God's infinite capacity to provide every failure, no matter how severe or destructive, with some value within the total scheme of things.[17]

A second corrective to Browning's approach may be found in the other major reflection upon the atonement from a process perspective, that of Daniel Day Williams.[18] Williams follows Josiah Royce in placing the meaning of Christ's death within the context of the entire community. "Royce sought to interpret human existence as the search for loyalty to an adequate cause. Sin is disloyalty to the one really adequate cause, the world of loyal men. . . . In its memory of Jesus the Church has the foundation of its existence in the memory of the deed of Jesus who acted in absolute loyalty to the community in the midst of its disloyalty.[19] Royce's analysis, however, needs to be deepened by an understanding of suffering, which Williams understands not so much in terms of undergoing pain as "being acted upon or being conformed to another in a relationship."[20] Such suffering appears to be identical with the empathic acceptance of those negativities of existence which usually cause pain and evil. To Royce's view Williams adds "the insight that the reconciliation which creates the new community comes by way of suffering. Jesus' suffering becomes the very word and speech of love finding bodily, historical expression and creating a new possibility of community."[21] This suffering, moreover, discloses God's own suffering to man. God's love is absolute in its integrity, invulnerable to any destruction, but this by no means implies any impassibility to suffering, which is at the heart of the most profound love. "If God does not suffer then his love is separated completely from the profoundest human experiences of love, and the suffering of Jesus is unintelligible as the communication of God's love to man."[22] Through such suffering reconciliation and renewal of love are effected (in ways more fully explored by Browning), bringing into existence a new community, the church, which Williams defines as "the community which lives by participation in the atonement."[23]

Here we find the clue indicating the intrinsic connection between the atonement and the resurrection, once we recognize that the church is none other than the resurrected body of Christ. Given our understanding of the way God acts in cooperative union with his creatures, we cannot see the resurrection as a unilateral action of God. On the one hand, raising Jesus to himself cannot simply be a purely arbitrary decision on God's part, but one made in response to the intrinsic quality of Jesus' life, suffering, and death. He is the one most worthy to be raised, because the living purpose of Jesus concretely embodied God's own purpose for mankind. Were any other person with a narrower outlook or sympathies raised up as the living source of aims to which we humans would be subordinate, we could find ourselves subject to a demonic totalitarianism destructive of the best possibilities inherent in us as separate individuals. A risen Christ to whom we can subordinate ourselves in good conscience must be one ''whom to serve is perfect freedom.'' Jesus can become that risen Christ only because his living purpose fulfills and does not thwart our highest aims. On the other hand, the resurrection of the body of Chirst also involves the transformation of individual men into willing members of that body, and this can only be effected through the atonement.

As Browning has shown, the function of atonement is to overcome those structures of sin which cause us to deny and distort the love of God in our lives. These structures arise from the absolutizing of those value-conditions given to us by God into conditions of acceptability whereby we judge our failures and worthlessness in such a way as to alienate ourselves from God's love. Moreover, these structures that tend to isolate us as individuals save as they bring us together in terms of the fairly rigid social patterns of ''life under the law.'' Before we can become members of the body of Christ, these structures must be broken down, in order to free us from limiting self-concepts, from the tendency to minimize and downgrade the values we aspire to in a desperate effort to avoid self-judgments of failure which accompany the acceptance of divine values. Given the greatly expanded resources at man's disposal, coupled with God's invariant aim at the maximum intensity and enrichment of experience, it is inevitable that the ordinary human achievement will fall short of its originally intended goal. The Christian recognition of original sin appreciates this gap between the initial aim envisioned by God and the final outcome achieved by man in every human event.

Low-level achievement may well be insensitive to this gap either because the original resources are too meager or because there is insufficient awareness of the aims as received from God. But any high-grade achievement depends upon richer resources and upon increasing awareness of these initial aims which in their vibrant intensity may well outrun the achievements they evoke. Therefore, for the very awareness of more intensive aims we must be reassured of our acceptability despite our failures. Reconciliation through atonement places our ultimate acceptability upon a different plane from the judgment of our success or failure in terms of our initial values, thereby enabling us to aspire to those values with greatly reduced risk. Until we are thereby enabled to aspire to the highest values available to us as individual human beings, we cannot be in a position to aspire to those values transcending ourselves which direct the activity of the whole body of Christ. Without atonement, therefore, the resurrection of Christ would not have been possible—for there would be no individual human beings capable of being transformed into members of that body.

Through participation in the body of Christ we continue to experience this concrete embodiment of divine love, for Christ accepts, cherishes, and affirms us in precisely the same manner in which we accept our own bodies. We have become part of him, and, just as we cannot, he cannot limit his selfhood merely to his mind, excluding the activity of his body. Our acceptability before God is no longer simply dependent upon our individual roles as separate human beings, for we have become part of Christ, and concretely participate in his acceptability before God. Jesus' suffering and death have inaugurated a process of reconciliation which continues its work of concretely exhibiting to us the love of God in the body of Christ's resurrection.

Throughout this discussion we have insisted upon God's suffering, in apparent contradiction of the common assumption that God dwells in unbroken bliss. This language has been unavoidable, in order to emphasize that God is totally involved in our lives, including the negativities of our experience. His happiness is not purchased by the exclusion of our misery. Nevertheless, there is merit in the ancient concern over the alleged heresy of Patripassianism. That concern is ill expressed in the usual protective doctrine that only part of the Godhead suffered, the Son but not the Father. How are we then to understand John's word that the Father so loved the world that he was willing to give up the Son (John 3:16)? Is this done at no cost to him? I take the deepest meaning of this concern to lie in the conviction that God is never defeated by evil. He can absorb all evil and overcome it. "He saves the world as it passes into the immediacy of his own life. It is the judgment of a tenderness which loses nothing that can be saved. It is also the judgment of a wisdom which uses what in the temporal world is mere wreckage."[24]

Evil lies in the mutual obstruction of things; their conflict and disharmony engender suffering and loss. No matter what the conflict, God possesses infinite conceptual resources in his primordial nature whereby an appropriate pattern can supplement these conflicting elements, thereby transforming them into a harmonious good. In themselves the elements conflict, but not as taken up into the larger texture of meaning.[25] This analogy appears distressingly feeble, but only because our human powers of aesthetic creativity are so feeble. We can reconcile conflicts by the addition of clarifying distinctions and imaginative constructs, but only theoretical, not actual conflicts. We can create harmony from discordant sounds by the addition of further sounds, but only in music. We can transform gross evil into tragic beauty, but only on the stage, only in make-believe, when the proper aesthetic distance has been achieved. Our powers of imaginative reconciliation are very restricted indeed. We should not underestimate the powers of an unlimited imagination to overcome the conflicts of finite actualities.

Our redemption is found not only in the assurance that our unacceptability is accepted, but that the evil inherent therein is transformed into lasting value, a good we can dimly appreciate. "For the perfected actuality passes back into the temporal world, and qualifies this world so that each temporal actuality includes it as an immediate fact of relevant experience. For the kingdom of God is with us today. . . . What is done in the world is transformed into a reality in heaven, and the reality in heaven passes back into the world. By reason of this reciprocal relation, the love in the world passes into the love in heaven, and floods back again into the world."[26] In the provision of novel aims for our ongoing activity, in the wellsprings of our renewed selfhood received afresh from above, God discloses the redemptive value whereby he cherishes our past. This sense of transformed meaning is very elusive, and exceedingly hard to describe. We can only refer the reader to the final chapter in *Adventures of Ideas*, in which Whitehead tries to explain this ultimate "Peace." We cannot hope to improve on his words.

Jesus had this "Peace," this assurance of ultimate victory throughout his life and ministry. It was what sustained his radical obedience, confirmed his quiet sense of authority, and encouraged him to address God as his father. Yet at the very end of his life this "Peace" deserted him: "My God, my God, why hast thou forsaken me?" (Mark 15:34). Jesus did not die a "good" death, with the serene nobility of a Socrates, but in the painful awareness that the intimate presence of God had been withdrawn in the ultimate hour, and he had been abandoned as one rejected. Jürgen Moltmann has recently underscored this forsakenness, challenging us to come to terms with this horrifying prospect. He argues that it can only be described in inner-trinitarian terms: "The abandonment on the cross which separates the Son from the Father is something which takes place within God himself.'"[27] Yet for the Son to be abandoned by the Father, there must be two distinct subjectivities within the Godhead. Many ontologies can permit this, but not Whitehead's. As we have seen in our discussion of Lionel Thornton's Christology any distinct subjectivity is necessarily a distinct actuality. Any doctrine suggesting three subjectivities within the Godhead automatically degenerates into tritheism. How, then, can we understand this abandonment, this radical bereavement Jesus felt?

As we have seen, the experience of redemptive love, "Peace," renewing life, is intimately bound up with the provision of initial aims. God is at work in every life providing it with novel aims at every turn, and Jesus was profoundly sensitive to this. Yet these aims, to be relevant, must express real possibilities for the moment; otherwise they could not be actualized under the circumstances. Each occasion of experience is free to actualize itself within the parameters of its causal past, but only within those parameters, since this past provides the content of its actualization. Normally the past allows us some leeway, but it can be coercive, restricting our future within very narrow confines. The initial aim articulates God's evaluative gift of these real possibilities, but they may be severely constrained. "The initial aim is the best for that *impasse*." But if the best be bad, Whitehead can speak of the ruthlessness of God.[28] In the hour of Jesus' deepest need, he could not feel the presence of God, because there were no redemptive possibilities that God could provide, no aims which could vouchsafe to him the infinite resourcefulness of the divine life in clothing his actions with resplendent meaning, sending him forth with renewed courage. For Jesus, there was only the cross and death. In his cross the weakness of God is revealed, as he stood by powerless to comfort his beloved. The worst of it was that God intimately experienced Jesus' awareness that this sustaining grace had suddenly been taken from him. God did not abandon Jesus, but he knew this abandonment, as Jesus knew it, in the depths of his being.

"What is inexorable in God," Whitehead continues, "is valuation as

an aim towards 'order'; and 'order' means 'society' permissive of actualities with patterned intensity of feeling arising from adjusted contrasts.''[29] This abstract description is very general, applying equally well
to molecules, amoeba, trees, rabbits, man, and that which transcends man
in some new transhuman organic society. The ruthlessness of God is
inexorable in evoking new intensities of being. Thus the very act in which
Jesus felt abandonment in his death enabled the emergence of the lure for
resurrection in the near future. In this transhuman body we need no longer
fear abandonment of God in death, for even that can contribute to ongoing
life. Jesus underwent the abandonment of God, so necessary for the
emergence of the resurrected body, in order that we might be spared this
experience.

As we have seen in the last chapter, this risen Christ is a living subjectivity, distinct from the divine subjectivity. In this our proposal has a
distinctly Arian flavor: Christ is temporally created, not begotten. On the
other hand, we also agree with Athanasius that the Logos, the second
member of the Trinity, is nontemporally begotten ''before all worlds.''
We can be both Arian and Athanasian by denying the one point they share
in common, namely, the identification of the risen Christ with the preexistent Logos. Here Arius errs philosophically in supposing this preexistent
Logos could be created in time and errs religiously in worshiping that
which is other than God. The living subjectivity of Christ is temporally
emergent, but not ''in the beginning,'' nor even in the birth or baptism of
Jesus. Jesus died so that Christ might be born. But Christ is not to be
worshiped in himself, but serves only as a mediator, magnifying the
availability of God to us. In him the divine aims for our lives can be
intensified in a way not possible without him. Yet the very fact that he is
our privileged means of access to God, such that only in Christ do we
encounter the fullness of God, should not blind us to the createdness and
relativity of even the risen Christ. There may be other transhuman
societies, in the future or even now, just as there may be other living
societies embracing intelligent life on other worlds, or even emergent
forms capable of incorporating the fullness of Christ within an unimagin-
able intensity and richness of being. The possibilities which the divine
creative Word holds for the future are inexhaustible, and any restriction of
that Word to the risen Christ bespeaks a parochial anthropocentrism we
should eschew.

Yet while the Christ is created, temporally emergent in the resurrection, he truly incarnates the Word of God addressed to our situation. His subjectivity is temporally emergent, yet the objective principle that he embodies relative to our need is grounded in the very fabric of the transcendent, primordial God. For the purpose of explicating this inner complexity of the Godhead the ancient doctrine of the Trinity is highly illuminating, as we shall see in the next chapter.

NOTES

1. John Courtney Murray, *The Problem of God* (New Haven: Yale University Press, 1964), pp. 25–29.

2. Gen. 6:6; Jer. 31:20; Isa. 63:15. Cf. Kazoh Kitamori, *The Theology of the Pain of God* (Richmond: John Knox Press, 1965).

3. Jürgen Moltmann, *The Crucified God* (New York: Harper & Row, 1974), esp. pp. 182ff.

4. *PR*, p. 521.

5. *Ibid.*, pp. 523–33.

6. *AI*, pp. 380–81.

7. *PR*, p. 521.

8. *Ibid.*, p. 533.

9. *Ibid.*, p. 373.

10. Don S. Browning, *Atonement and Psychotherapy* (Philadelphia: Westminster Press, 1966).

11. *Ibid.*, p. 101.

12. *Ibid.*, p. 194.

13. *Ibid.*, p. 230.

14. *Ibid.*, p. 201.

15. Browning bases his study on Hartshorne's process theism, and it is appropriate to interpret his theory of the divine imposition of the laws of nature in terms of coercion. Cf. Charles Hartshorne, *A Natural Theology for Our Time* (La Salle, Ill.: Open Court, 1967), pp. 101–2, 120. Yet this need not be the case if, as Whitehead argues, the laws of nature summarize the average response of the creatures to divine persuasion. On this difference between Hartshorne and Whitehead, see *Two Process Philosophers*, ed. Lewis S. Ford (American Academy of Religion: AAR Studies in Religion 5, 1973), pp. 75–79.

16. *PR*, p. 517.

17. See also Browning's argument, *Atonement and Psychotherapy*, pp. 149–53, that the effectiveness of psychotherapeutic acceptance depends upon a wider context of divine acceptance, which we would argue is in turn justified by God's capacity to infuse anything with imaginative value.

18. Daniel Day Williams, *The Spirit and the Forms of Love* (New York: Harper & Row, 1968), pp. 173–91.

19. *Ibid.*, pp. 180–81.

20. *Ibid.*, p. 182.

21. *Ibid.*, p. 184.

22. *Ibid.*, p. 185.

23. *Ibid.*, p. 188.

24. *PR*, p. 525. These words are easily misunderstood as meaning that there is some residue of unredeemable evil that God cannot overcome. Yet all *being*, no matter how evil and recalcitrant, can be saved; it is *becoming* that cannot be preserved, for becoming necessarily ceases ("perishes") in the attainment of being. The indeterminacy of becoming is replaced by the determinateness of being.

25. See my essay on divine persuasion, cited in Chapter 3, note 22.

26. *PR*, p. 532.

27. Moltmann, *The Crucified God,* pp. 151–52. See the whole context, pp. 146–53.

28. *PR*, p. 373.

29. *Ibid.*, pp. 373–74.

CHAPTER 7

A Process Trinitarianism

Trinitarian reflection has fallen on evil days. At one point in the history of the Christian faith it formed the cutting edge of theological speculation, responding to the need to clarify the relationship between its two central symbols, "Christ" and "God." Then under the threat of heresy and schism this reflection crystallized into dogma, becoming no longer the object and goal of reflection, but a bit of permanent cultural baggage whose continued presence had to be explained and rationalized. In recent times many have sought to justify trinitarian formulations by employing them for the articulation of God's simultaneous transcendence of, and immanence in, the world. Increasingly, however, the artificiality of these attempts is being called into question, for it is by no means evident that this problem demands a triunity of principles for its resolution. Thus Cyril C. Richardson has criticized the classical formulations of the Trinity as imposing an arbitrary "threeness" upon our theological thinking, and proposes instead a basic twofold distinction between God as Absolute and God as Related.[1] This is for Richardson a basic paradox, an apparent self-contradiction, for if we try to bring these aspects into relationship, we compromise God's absoluteness.[2] Charles Hartshorne accepts this same twofold distinction, but he removes the contradictory element by understanding it in terms of the abstract and concrete dimensions of God's nature and experience.[3]

Classical theism sees only a single problem here, the question of God's transcendence and immanence, for which a twofold solution is quite adequate. From the perspective of Whitehead's theism, however, there is a double problem, the other aspect consisting in the world's transcendence of, and immanence within, God. Only a trinitarian conception of

God seems able to meet this problem. Trinitarian speculation may have spoken more wisely than it knew by providing the basic coordinates for a problem which did not even arise within the horizon of classical theism. Like conic sections, which had to wait nearly two thousand years for their first important application in Kepler's description of the elliptical orbits of the planets, perhaps the trinitarian conceptuality, at least with regard to the problem of transcendence and immanence, first comes into its own in our situation. If God's relation to the world necessarily entails a fundamental triunity, this triunity may provide the conceptual means for coordinating our contemporary understanding of the key biblical symbols.

Some conclusions about the Trinity and the workings of God have already emerged from earlier chapters. We have seen that God works by divine persuasion by providing those lures toward which we can aspire. Jesus proclaimed this reigning of God as the power of the future operative in the present. Insofar as we respond to actualize these aims, to that extent the good is achieved in creative advance. To that extent God is effective in our lives.

Divine persuasion is not limited, however, solely to human beings. It extends to the entire created order, and constitutes the means whereby God directs the evolutionary process, both here and on distant planets. It addresses both subhuman creatures and extraterrestrial intelligent species, each after its own kind.

Here we need a series of distinctions: The *Logos* is the totality of the divine aims, both large and small, relevant and irrelevant. Those aims capable of addressing an entire species by infusing in them a novel order bringing about the emergence of a more advanced species constitute that part of the Logos which we call the *creative Word*. That creative Word which is specifically addressed to humankind is the *Christ*. Christians find this creative Word most fully actualized in the life, death, and resurrection of Jesus as they participate in that body whose living mind they discern to be the risen Christ.

Too often these distinctions have been ignored with the result that the preexistent subjectivity of Jesus is identified with the second member of the Trinity. Surely this is the assumption of the Fourth Gospel (cf. John 17:1–5). But, as we have seen, there cannot be distinct subjectivities within the Godhead. On Whitehead's principles, whatever has actual unity enjoys its own subjectivity, and vice versa. Thus a divine person enjoying his own subjectivity would be a separate actuality, thus leading to tritheism. Moreover, substance in the sense of a divine substratum in which three persons inhere is just that sort of vacuous actuality devoid of its own subjectivity that Whitehead rejects. For these reasons we cannot accept the traditional Latin interpretation of the time-honored formula, "one substance in three persons," and insist on a stricter reading more in accordance with the Greek fathers, "one actuality having three distinct aspects." Originally *per-sona* did not mean "person" in our sense but the mask through which an actor spoke, indicating the specific role he was performing. The three "personae" come from the three roles God plays. These roles are not arbitrary, however, but are rooted in the very being of God. In the language of Duns Scotus, these natures are formally distinct. They are not really distinct, for this would imply the possibility of separate existence, nor are they merely logically distinct.

Christ enjoys his own subjectivity, to be sure, but only in his resurrection, not in some preexistent state. The risen Christ is divine in the sense of being that transparent medium which most intensely communicates God's aims to the Christian. But in himself the risen Christ is more transhuman than divine. As a possibility, Christ is that aspect of the creative Word addressed to man, and hence part of the Logos. But as actualized in the resurrection of Jesus that possibility becomes a temporally emergent subjectivity separate from God.

In order to address the trinitarian conceptuality directly, then, we need to consider the formal distinction between the Father and the Logos. As the totality of divine possibilities, the Logos may be interpreted as corresponding to the primordial nature of God. As Whitehead conceives it, the primordial nature embraces all eternal objects as the source from whence all initial aims for finite occasions are derived. This primordial nature is also the outcome of a single nontemporal concrescence. As such it corresponds to the Logos as identical with the Son who is "begotten of the Father before all worlds."

According to the Nicene Creed the Son is begotten, not made. This protective formula indicates that the Son is of the same substance as the Father. This does not merely mean that they share a common "material" substratum, as we have seen, but they are aspects of the selfsame actuality. Nevertheless, the second is produced from the first. We have a very close parallel in Whitehead's general distinction between the two aspects of an actual entity. On the one hand, there is the act of becoming, that process of unification which is the concrescence or growing together of causal influences. On the other hand, there is the being constituted by this becoming, the unity produced by this unification, the concrete satisfaction, or what has been called the "concretum" of this concrescence.[4] The concrescence "begets" the concretum in this metaphysical sense that it produces it as a formally distinct aspect of its own actuality.

Moreover, in the divine instance this concrescence is nontemporal, independent of the particular temporal passage of the world. "Before all worlds," as Augustine recognized, symbolically refers to an activity outside of time, whether or not the world had a temporal beginning. Time is part of the world, and there is no time "before" the world in which such begetting could take place. That which is nontemporally "begotten" is itself outside of the time, an atemporal Logos of the many eternal objects.[5]

Trinitarian thinking has always labored under a difficulty with respect to God as Father: on the one hand, according to the classical formula, God the Father can only constitute one person of the Trinity; on the other, the Father whom Jesus addressed is simply God, particularly God as revealed to Israel. Part of the difficulty stems from the temptation to believe that God in Christ constitutes a second divine subjectivity distinct from the Father's, both of which must be united in the Trinity to preserve at least the semblance of monotheism. The rest results from the failure to develop a general theory of immanence whereby one actuality could be recognized as being present objectively within the experience of another without thereby destroying its integrity as a distinct individual actuality.[6] In contrast to Aristotle's dictum that one substance (i.e., actuality) cannot be in another, Whitehead's philosophy is designed to show how this may be so. One actuality, as concretum, can be objectively present in the concrescence of another. The concrescence is the actuality in its transcendent hiddenness; as such it cannot be experienced by another; the concretum is its objective manifestation. The one nontemporal concrescence is God's innermost subjectivity by which he radically transcends the world. In Plotinus's terms, it is the unknowable "One" which is the source of the eternal generation. We can only know of it insofar as it is expressed in the primordial nature, for in itself it is God in his hiddenness, in the inexhaustible mystery of his being.

Perhaps, as John Cobb suggests, the mischief is wrought by conceiving of God the Father as a distinct persona in the Godhead. "The actual image was of the Son as God in one mode of his activity and the Spirit as God in another mode, whereas the Father was quite simply God."[7] The metaphysical distinction between that which is hidden in itself and that which is manifest for others is hardly enough to have caused any departure from the strict monotheism of the Old Testament heritage. Israel was acquainted with the manifestations of God as his Spirit, but this did not suggest that God in his inner being constituted one divine person distinct from the Spirit of the Lord. The trinitarian distinctions were called forth by the fact that the Christian community recognized two distinctive manifestations of God in the Logos, in part incarnated by Christ, and the all-pervasive Spirit. In early Christian art this Trinity could be portrayed as a man with two hands. In Whiteheadian terms, we may interpret God in his full unified actuality as a transcendent subjectivity, which is manifest in two natures, one primordial and the other consequent. There is no need to introduce a third distinct nature on a par with these two.[8] "God the Father" is simply God, not another member within the Godhead.

This consequent nature of God is his receptive activity whereby he experiences the temporal occasions of the world. Here our interpretation is somewhat tentative, because we must recognize that any simple identification of the Spirit with this consequent nature will only produce confusion. In a very real sense the Spirit and the consequent nature are opposites, since the Spirit makes it possible for God to be immanent in the world (in the guise of ordinary divine aims), while the consequent nature makes it possible for the world to be immanent in God (through God's ongoing experience of that temporal world). Nevertheless, it is by means of our experience of successive divine aims provided by the Spirit that we have any evidence (howbeit indirect) for the existence of God's consequent nature.

Before explaining this evidence, however, we need to be clear about the activity of the Spirit. Spirit and Logos both concern the provision of initial aims, since that is the only way God is manifest to us. Logos, however, concentrates upon *what* is so provided, particularly the great structuring principles of the world and of particular species. Spirit describes *how* these aims are given, and its activities are best seen in the little, ordinary aims we receive from day to day.

The Spirit is the Lord and Giver of Life in providing those novel aims that organisms can actualize in living response to a dynamic environment. We humans are primarily aware of the aims of the Spirit in terms of ethical aspiration, so vividly present in the Hebrew prophets. Creative insight is also "inspired," for genuine discovery is directed toward a novel possibility hitherto unrealized in the world. Finally, it is by means of the Spirit that we can learn to respond consciously to God, since it is through the awareness of values first purposefully entertained by God that we are directed to seek out their divine source.

We cannot directly experience God's experience of us, but the particular aims he supplies to our ongoing experience form his specific response to our past actions. Most of the time, preoccupied with practical affairs, we hardly notice the aims and values which guide our activities. Occasionally we may become sensitive to these values, but usually as directives for our own existence, as moral intuitions. Only rarely do we experience these values in terms of the dynamic source from which they spring. Such "religious intuitions" are the "somewhat exceptional elements of our conscious experience" that Whitehead seeks to elucidate as evidence for God's consequent experience of the world.[9] Only a living person experiencing a whole series of divine aims, sensitive to the way in which these shift, grow, and develop in response to our changing circumstances can become aware of their source as dynamic and personal, meeting our needs and concerns.[10] Jesus, full of the Spirit, knew God personally in this intimate way, until these aims were taken from him in the hour of his deepest need, when he experienced being forsaken by God on the cross.

This awareness of God's consequent experience is highly indirect, but this is equally true for our experience of any subjectivity other than our own. We can detect no subjectivity in inorganic societies, and little more in living societies such as plants or animal tissues. We only gain confidence in our sense of the presence of other feeling subjects when dealing with the focalized mental activity of the higher animals and human beings. Here all our experiential evidence is indirect, but reliable. We feel the presence of another person in his actions, for we experience those actions as living responses to ourselves and our actions. There can be an exchange of feeling, because I can experience his action *as* his responsive experience of me. So it is with the Spirit, which can bear witness to God's responsive experience of his creatures.

Because of their distinct roles in the providing of initial aims, Logos and Spirit thus reflect the two distinct natures of God, the primordial and the consequent. But just as "person" in trinitarian language has caused confusion, so Whitehead's use of a distinction of reason in referring to these two divine "natures" has led to misunderstanding. Few careful readers have supposed the primordial and consequent natures to be separate divine actualities,[11] yet there has been a tendency to consider each nature as having its own distinctive functions, each operating with some degree of independence from the other.[12] But this is ultimately not the case. The primordial nature is the source of all those possible ideals which can serve as the initial aims of occasions, while God's consequent experience of the actual world forms the basis whereby God can specify which aims are relevant for which occasions, thereby serving as "the particular providence for particular occasions."[13]

This proposal differs from traditional trinitarian formulations in that the third principle indicated by Spirit does not have the primary function of unifying the other two. In part this role is unnecessary. In one sense this unity is provided by the first member, the aboriginal nontemporal act from which all aspects of God are generated. In another sense the unity lies in their mutual coherence; each is merely an aspect requiring the others to constitute the one divine individual actuality. The nontemporal activity must result in some sort of definite, atemporal unity, while the primordial nature must be the outcome of some sort of nontemporal activity. They are implicates of one another, as process and outcome, as act and expression, as dynamics and form. Moreover, God must be capable of experiencing the world if he is to exemplify the metaphysical principles contained in his primordial nature resulting from that nontemporal act. But beyond this, the consequent nature does not have unification as its primary function because it is needed for a different role, called forth by the problematic of transcendence and immanence.

To see why this is so, we must consider the particular meaning that Whitehead assigns to transcendence. It is a generic notion, not a specific notion applicable only to God. "The transcendence of God is not peculiar to him. Every actual entity, in virtue of its novelty, transcends its universe, God included."[14] "Every actual entity, including God, is something individual for its own sake; and thereby transcends the rest of actuality."[15] Each actuality goes beyond the world it inherits, for it is something more than the components from which it is constituted. It is the free creative unification of the many past actualities it experiences, thereby becoming something more than what has already existed, something individual for its own sake. Such transcendence is possible only because of the incessant creative urge transforming every multiplicity as it arises into an actual unity. "The creativity is not an external agency with its own ulterior purposes. All actual entities share with God this characteristic of transcending all other actual entities, including God. The universe is thus a creative advance into novelty."[16] As an ongoing activity, creativity is not exhausted in the transcendence of any one actuality: "every actual entity, including God, is a creature transcended by the creativity which it qualifies."[17]

God, however, transcends and is transcended in ways peculiar to him. A finite actuality or occasion of experience exhausts its creativity (its only power of transcendence) in a momentary act of self-unification, to be superseded by others. God draws all actualities into an inexhaustible unity, since the inner aim informing divine creativity and impelling it forward is infinite, seeking the realization of every possibility, each in its own season. A finite occasion's transcendence is relative, transcending its past but not its future. God's transcendent creativity is absolute, transcending every actuality as it arises by incorporating it into his being. On the other hand, finite occasions are absolutely transcended by subsequent actualities, having no other being than that afforded by their objective status in the transcendent creativity. God is only partially transcended by actual occasions, for they can only prehend those aims of God relevant to their particular world, leaving untouched those infinite reservoirs of possibility which are not yet (or no longer) relevant to the creative advance.

Now it may be objected that this notion of transcendence does not do justice to God's ultimacy. Here we must distinguish between metaphysical and religious meanings for ultimacy. Whitehead had the first in mind when he wrote: "In all philosophic theory there is an ultimate which is actual in virtue of its accidents . . . . In the philosophy of organism this ultimate is termed 'creativity'; and God is its primordial, nontemporal accident."[18] God is an accident of creativity because the particular character of the primordial envisagement is not determined by the essential nature of creativity. Creativity only requires *that* the many become one, but *how* they become one is the decision of that actuality in process of self-creation. Creativity is metaphysically ultimate as the power of transcendence every actuality instantiates, including God. But this does not make it ultimate in the religious sense of being supremely worthy of worship.

Sheer creativity is utterly formless, essentially indifferent to all its instantiations, whether good or evil. Creativity acquires actuality only through these instantiations, which determine their own value. We should worship only that which is the ultimate source of human good, that one instance of creativity which orders all value. Borrowing Spinoza's language, this divine creative act is *natura naturans,* God as creating, which issues forth as *natura naturata,* God as created, since he creates himself. The infinite "world" that God creates in creating himself is not, as Spinoza supposed, the world of determinate actuality, which is incurably finite, but the infinite wealth of structured possibility which constitutes God's primordial nature.

Appreciating the ultimacy of creativity in its metaphysical sense, some have suggested a trinity composed of creativity as the divine ground of being, the primordial nature as the divine Logos, and the consequent nature as the unifying Spirit. Such a proposal bears striking resemblances to Tillich's sketch of the trinitarian principles in terms of power, meaning, and their union.

> Human intuition of the divine always has distinguished between the abyss of the divine (the element of power) and the fullness of its content (the element of meaning), between the divine depth and the divine *logos.* The first principle is the basis of Godhead, that which makes God God. It is the root of his majesty, the unapproachable intensity of his being, the inexhaustible ground of being in which everything has its origin. It is the power of being infinitely resisting nonbeing, giving the power of being to everything that is.[19]

This is certainly the role of creativity.

Whitehead, however, sees God in his transcendent role as that portion of creativity embodied within the divine creative act, reserving the rest of creativity for finite creative acts. Both thinkers begin with a dynamic, radically indeterminate source of being, called creativity or being-itself, but proceed according to different models of creation: Tillich adopts the traditional dichotomy between an uncreated creator and created creatures, and identifies creativity with this creator, while Whitehead envisages a multiplicity of self-created creatures, all instances of creativity, among whom God is chief. This second approach has two principal advantages: it protects the goodness of God, and insures the freedom of his fellow creatures.

If God were ultimately creativity or being-itself, he would be radically indeterminate, and no theory of symbolic predication can finally overcome this.[20] As Tillich recognizes, "Without the second principle the first principle would be chaos, burning fire, but it would not be the creative ground."[21] Only as structured by the Logos can creativity become divine. Apart from the primordial envisagement, divine creativity is indistinguishable from creativity in general, and the tendency toward pantheism in which Brahma replaces Yahweh becomes inevitable. Apart from the envisagement of the forms, creativity is "chaos, burning fire," the divine-demonic power that the prophets of Israel struggled against in declaring Yahweh to be a God of justice. God cannot be sheer creativity, but only that creative act which supremely exemplifies the metaphysical principles.

Granted that creativity must to some extent be structured by the divine Logos, is it exhaustively or solely structured by it? If so, we end up with deterministic Spinozism. If creativity is not exhausted in producing the Logos, there can be creaturely freedom, but by the same token there can be no simple identification of divinity with creativity.

From Whitehead's perspective, God's creative act (in terms of its relevant aspects in the initial aim) can be objectively present within the finite occasion's concrescence, for it is now the creaturely response which must synthesize the divine and mundane causes it receives into a determinate unity. To effect this synthesis the creature must enjoy its own intrinsic creativity distinct from the divine creativity it objectively receives. It is precisely this dissociation of creativity from God which renders finite transcendence possible, for it allows creativity to be conceived pluralistically rather than monistically, as underwriting every act of freedom, both finite and infinite. The creativity which is not God becomes the radical freedom of self-creation over against God.

If, then, there is creative activity which does not stem from God, how can God embrace it? This is the question which calls forth the role of the consequent nature. If effects produce themselves out of their causes, then it becomes more important that we conceive of God as the supreme effect than as the supreme cause. The whole world supplies the contingent, particular causes of which God is the supreme unification in his consequent experience. In creating he knows himself as the infinitude of all pure possibility, but he does not thereby know finite determinate temporal actuality. To that extent he is dependent upon contingent actuality for the content of his knowledge and experience, although the unity and final intelligibility of that divine experience derives from his own powers of unification. God's knowledge of the world is finite, temporal, and contingent because the world is so, and this knowledge cannot be derived either from God's nontemporal act or its atemporal outcome in the primordial nature. Another principle is required, and this is consequent nature which has the capacity to receive into itself the objective immanence of the world.

Classical theism in effect sees a single problem: it is as true to say that God transcends the world, as that God is immanent in the world. This problem may be adequately resolved by a twofold distinction, such as that proposed by Richardson and Hartshorne: God as Absolute and God as Related. But, as Whitehead saw, there is a double problem which he expressed in a pair of terse antitheses: "It is as true to say that the World is immanent in God, as that God is immanent in the World. It is as true to say that God transcends the World, as that the World transcends God."[22] Our twofold distinction explains how God transcends and yet is immanent within God.

Classical theism sees no problem in the immanence of the world within God, primarily because it refuses to grant the world any transcendence from God. In terms of the traditional model, the creature derives all of his being and power from God, even his power of opposition and disobedience. Insofar as God knows by creating, the creature is already immanent within God. The creature can only transcend God if it can become something in and for itself independently of God, in the privacy of its own subjective becoming. The world transcends God on its own, but its subsequent immanence within God requires an additional element of receptive dependence within God. For God is dependent upon the independent, transcendent activity of the creature for knowledge and experience of it. The problem of God's simultaneous transcendence and immanence alone requires only a twofold distinction, but the additional problem of the world's simultaneous transcendence and immanence calls forth an additional element, making a final threefold distinction necessary.

Thus in the final analysis we must assent to an ultimate triunity of principles defining the divine life: the divine creative act nontemporally generating the primordial nature, from which proceeds the consequent nature as implicated in the Whiteheadian "categoreal conditions" established by the primordial envisagement.

NOTES

1. Cyril C. Richardson, *The Doctrine of the Trinity* (Nashville: Abingdon Press, 1958).

2. *Ibid.*, pp. 8–9.

3. See Charles Hartshorne, "God as Absolute, Yet Related to All," chapter 2 of *The Divine Relativity* (New Haven: Yale University Press, 1948).

4. See George L. Kline, "Form, Concrescence, and Concretum," *Southern Journal of Philosophy* 7/4 (Winter 1969–70), 351–60.

5. Here see my essay on "The Non-Temporality of Whitehead's God," *International Philosophical Quarterly* 13/3 (September 1973), 347–76.

6. As we saw in the first chapter, Whitehead argues that the Nicene fathers developed just such a theory of direct immanence, but then failed to generalize it, restricting it to the one instance of God's immanence in Christ.

7. *CPA*, pp. 259–60.

8. To be sure, there is also a single, brief mention of "the 'superjective' nature of God" (*PR*, p. 135). Some have supposed this to refer to a third distinct nature, such that the proper Whiteheadian trinity consists of the primordial, consequent, and superjective natures. In context, however, the 'superjective' nature of God is formed on strict analogy with the superjective character of other actual entities, and refers to the objective immanence of the primordial nature in the initial aims of actual occasions.

The two natures appear under other guises in Whitehead's later writings, but no further reference is ever made to any additional superjective nature. Thus in *Adventures of Ideas* he contrasts the divine "Eros" with "the Adventure in the Universe as One" (pp. 380–81), which in *Modes of Thought* (New York: Macmillan, 1938) he refers to as "the reservoir of potentiality and the coordination of achievement" (p. 128).

Whitehead announces that "the objective immortality of [God's] consequent nature" is considered in part V of *Process and Reality* (p. 47), which appears to have reference to the fourth phase considered at the end of the book (p. 532). The reference is very brief, and seems fraught with difficulties. Only that which is complete, either as a completely definite primordial nature, or as a completely determinate actual occasion, can be objectified. But the consequent nature is never complete, since there are always new occasions for God to prehend. As we shall see, however, Spirit can fulfill the role assigned to this fourth phase of being "the particular providence for particular occasions" (*PR*, p. 532). In any case, there is no basis in the text for associating the "superjective" nature with the objectification of the consequent nature.

9. *PR*, p. 521.

10. For this reason Whitehead speaks of "the perishing occasions in the life of each temporal Creature" (*PR*, p. 533), referring to living persons and not simply to individual

actual occasions. See also his comment that "this account of a living personality requires completion by reference to its objectification in the consequent nature of God" (*PR*, p. 164, n. 17.)

11. Yet Oliver Martin has managed to do just that: "Whitehead's Naturalism and God," *Review of Religion* 3 (1939), 149–60.

12. John W. Lansing cites several instances of this tendency, the most striking being: "The actual entity that is needed to order the possibilities is called the primordial nature of God." This statement is excerpted from Victor Lowe, *Understanding Whitehead* (Baltimore: The Johns Hopkins University Press, 1962), p. 101. See Lansing's article, "The 'Natures' of Whitehead's God," *Process Studies* 3/3 (Fall 1973), 143–52.

13. *PR*, p. 532. See note 8 above.

14. *Ibid.*, p. 143.

15. *Ibid.*, p. 135.

16. *Ibid.*, pp. 339–40.

17. *Ibid.*, p. 135; cf. pp. 130, 134, 339.

18. *Ibid.*, pp. 10–11.

19. Paul Tillich, *Systematic Theology*, vol. 1 (Chicago: The University of Chicago Press, 1951), pp. 250–51.

20. I defend this claim in "Tillich and Thomas: The Analogy of Being," *Journal of Religion* 46/2 (April 1966), 229–45.

21. Tillich, *Systematic Theology* 1, p. 251.

22. *PR*, p. 528.

CHAPTER 8

The Sources of
Christian Hope

Pierre Teilhard de Chardin has been perhaps the most eloquent apostle of
Christian hope in recent years, discerning in the evolutionary process an
increasing convergence and complexification that will finally result in the
Omega point, the consummation and terminus of history foreshadowed in
Jesus as the Christ. Yet how can we be certain that this final convergence
will yield the full personalization of man instead of his collectivization or
destruction? Does God guarantee a final victory? Can we have the confidence that God will finally bring about the triumph of good, no matter
how badly we fail him? If so, its coming is inevitable, and we need not
strive to bring it about. Then the risks of this world lose their seriousness, for there is no ultimate risk. If the good triumphs no matter what,
the sufferings that God allows us to endure on the way lose their meaning
because he could have accomplished his purposes without them.

But what if, on the other hand, there is no final triumph of good, and
we simply face the bleak prospect of more of the same? It is all too easy to
dismiss Teilhard as a facile optimist, without penetrating to the root of his
desperate vision. Teilhard was deeply sensitive to the growing hopeless-
ness of modern man. Without the assurance of tomorrow, can we go on
living? Hope releases the energies of man, and the lure of a better future is
the only reason for any striving. Individual, particular, proximate hopes,
however, must be situated within an horizon of ultimate hope. For all the
hopes and strivings of man are unmasked as utter vanity if the final end of
the universe is simply a wasting away into nothingness.

The logic of the situation seems inexorable: without hope, we are lost
and still in our sins. This hope requires an ultimate horizon which must be
both real and good, for otherwise our hope is based on an illusion. But an

inevitable triumph of good undercuts the seriousness and risk of the human task, and gives the lie to its manifold sufferings.

Here metaphysics fails us. Any metaphysical necessity that might be adduced to give us confidence in our future would be too heavy-handed. We would simply be reduced to passive spectators before its inexorability. As Paul wrote, "Hope that is seen is not hope. For who hopes for what he sees?" (Rom. 8:24). That which we "see" by metaphysical insight should be included under this ban. Hope means trust in a future which is to be acted out in our deeds and efforts. Metaphysics may enable us to see whether this trust is reasonable, but it cannot be its basis.

Hence in this chapter we must leave metaphysical certainties and venture forth tentatively, sketching possible alternatives about which no final decisions can be made, exploring the bases of hope, first for ourselves, as grounded in the possible survival after death, and/or in the ongoing life of God, and then our hope for the future of the world.

In Whitehead's philosophy the soul is a series of momentary events or actual occasions supported by the body (particularly the brain) and coordinating its activities. It is not an enduring substance and does not necessarily survive the death of the body, as most have interpreted Plato to teach. On the other hand, Whitehead's metaphysics does not preclude such survival. "It is entirely neutral on the question of immortality, or on the existence of purely spiritual beings other than God."[1]

Subsequent process theologians have been deeply divided on this point. Charles Hartshorne[2] in *The Logic of Perfection* and Schubert Ogden[3] in "The Meaning of Christian Hope" have forcefully argued against any subjective immortality, holding that as objectively experienced by God our lives are wholly preserved and cherished forever. Without denying this objective immortality, David Griffin has examined the possibility of subjective survival more positively,[4] and John Cobb has speculated about the possible interpenetration of such souls in the hereafter in ways that overcome their possible self-centeredness.[5] Marjorie Suchocki has also explored ways in which we may live on in God which are quite different from these conceptions of the immortality of the soul.[6]

I find disembodied survival questionable, simply because the soul is so dependent upon the body. The body is its means for sensing and perceiving. All of its action is expressed through the body it coordinates. Quite probably all of its memory, and other subconscious activities, are provided for the soul by subordinate living occasions within the brain. Bereft of all these capacities, the soul might still be able to exist, but in such an impoverished state that it hardly seems worthwhile.

The situation might be quite different if the ongoing life of God were to provide the support for these continuing occasions of the soul which it had been accustomed to receive from the body. Whitehead briefly speculated on this possibility:

> How far this soul finds a support for its existence beyond the body is:— another question. The everlasting nature of God, which in a sense is non-temporal and in another sense is temporal, may establish with the soul a peculiarly intense relationship of mutual immanence. Thus in some important sense the existence of the soul may be freed from its complete dependence upon the bodily organization.[7]

In that case God might mediate to the soul the memory of past experiences from his own experiences of those events, and possibly even his perception of present events. God could also mediate the free actions of such souls to one another, taking care to harmonize any potential conflicts by means of conceptual supplementation, thus overcoming any evil consequent upon the free actions of many actualities acting in concert. On earth these free actions are communicated directly to supervening occasions, creating the risk of conflict and evil. But this freedom may well be possible within the perfect harmony of heaven, if God can neutralize the potential outcomes before they are able to produce any conflict.[8]

But is such subjective immortality needed? There seem to be three factors which impel man to look for life beyond the grave: (1) the preservation of values achieved, (2) the redemption from evil and suffering, (3) and the nonacceptance of the extinction of the self. Let us consider each of these factors in turn.

The first is the most insistent. What is the point of it all if it all ends in nothing? Our achievements may live on in the memories of others, but this is a very fragmentary and transient immortality. Eventually they too shall perish, as well as all traces of our existence. It is only a matter of time. If we survive death, then what we have experienced and achieved will survive with us. But to what extent? Rilke suggests that such earthly experiences and achievements would be remembered like the discarded playthings of our childhood, if at all. If, however, God perfectly remembers all that has happened, or better, is still experiencing in his ongoing, everlasting present whatever is past to us, the values we now cherish will be better preserved in the divine experience than they would be in any subjective immortality we might enjoy. Our own personal immortality is not needed, if all our achieved values are objectively immortal as cherished within the divine everlasting experience.

The second reason, concerning redemption from evil, really has two aspects. On the one hand, we may ask whether the guilty can be received by God; on the other, whether there can be any recompense for the suffering of the innocent.

Some interpret the saying that God's experience ''is the judgment of a tenderness which loses nothing that can be saved''[9] as meaning that God only preserves that which is good, discarding the evil as incapable of such preservation. That interpretation ignores the very next sentence: "It is also the judgment of a wisdom which uses what in the temporal world is *mere wreckage.*"[10] It also ignores the teaching of the apostle Paul, that we sinners are justified by grace, that we are accepted despite our unacceptability. If only the good that we do is received into God's experience, then most of what we are would be forever lost. God experiences all that we are and do, even though much of that causes conflict, evil, and suffering, not only to others but also to God.

This is all possible within the divine experience because God has all the inexhaustible resources of conceptual possibility to heal the wounds inflicted by actuality. Here we may gain a dim impression of Whitehead's point by recourse to works of the imagination. Art and poetry can transform the dull, ugly, irritating commonplaces of life into vibrant, meaningful realities by inserting them within fresh and unexpected contexts. The dramatic insight of a Sophocles can suffuse the grossly evil deeds of Oedipus the king with high tragedy by skillfully weaving these actions with choric commentary into an artful whole. These deeds would be horribly shocking to witness in actuality, yet in the drama this evil is transformed into tragic beauty. Likewise, the disciplined imagination of speculative reason can surmount the interminable conflicts between man and nature, mind and body, freedom and determinism, religion and science, by assigning each its rightful place within a larger systematic framework. The larger pattern, introduced conceptually, can bring harmony to discord by interrelating potentially disruptive elements in constructive ways. Since God's conceptual feelings as derived from his primordial nature are infinite, he has all the necessary resources to supplement his physical feelings perfectly, thereby achieving a maximum of intensity and harmony from every situation.

We may object that imagination is not enough. Certainly it is not enough in *our* experience. Our limited imaginations are easily overwhelmed by the insistent persistence of determinate actuality. But such actuality is itself limited. Could it not in turn be overcome and transformed by an infinite, inexhaustible, divine imagination?

This is a redemption that God experiences, but do *we* experience it? We could, if there were an objective immortality of the consequent nature.[11] Then it would be true that "the perfected actuality passes back into the temporal world, and qualifies this world so that each temporal actuality includes it as an immediate fact of relevant experience."[12] But God's everlasting concrescence would have to be completed for it to pass back into our world, and it is never complete. Whitehead never attempted to resolve this problem, and it is not clear that it could ever be solved.[13]

In the closing chapter of *Adventures of Ideas*, Whitehead discusses the final ideal requisite for the perfection of life, "Peace." It involves the tragic beauty that God creatively experiences in redeeming the world from evil, but it is not the direct experience of this redemption. Peace "is primarily a *trust* in the efficacy of Beauty."[14] We trust, without directly experiencing, this Beauty as that which ultimately makes it all worthwhile.

But is this enough? Coupled with the refusal to accept the extinction of the self is our frequent craving for the direct experience of compensation for any innocent suffering we have endured; if not now, at least in some life to come. But is this not a sign of that "restless egotism" that Peace is designed to overcome?[15]

It might be thought a just precept that each one should suffer for his own sins. This runs counter to the whole of Christian experience, however, rooted in the image of the suffering servant of the Lord depicted in Isaiah 53 as suffering on behalf of the sins of others. It runs counter to the meaning of Jesus' death as disclosing to us the depths of God's solidarity with the world, that he suffers the pain and destruction caused by the evil we inflict. Even though God is able to transform this suffering into joy by imaginatively suffusing its evil with tragic beauty, the fact remains that his initial experience of the world involves all the pain and loss that the conflict of its many actualities produces. God cannot ignore this conflict by blunting his perceptions, and he is acutely aware of the clash between what actually is and what might or ought to have been.

It might just be barely possible to insist upon this precept that each should suffer for the evil he inflicts, if the self endured to experience the result of its own actions and decisions. But within a Whiteheadian cosmology built upon momentary occasions, this is not possible. No occasion ever experiences the outcome of its own actions. What it experiences is bequeathed to it by others, for good or ill, and the results of its decision affect subsequent occasions, never itself. What we as momentary selves experience can never be that which we have done.

The quest for subjective immortality may simply be a disguised affirmation of the substantial, enduring self of traditional thought. Whitehead's meditation upon Peace combats this tendency. It is the quest for a Harmony of Harmonies that can utterly transcend the limits of any self. "It results in a wider sweep of conscious interest. It enlarges the field of attention. Thus Peace is self-control at its widest—at the width where the 'self' has been lost, and interest has been transferred to coordinations wider than personality."[16] If every self is thoroughly bound up with the past world it experiences, and the coming world it affects, so that it is constantly drawn out of itself to the other, this widening of concern beyond the self is most salutary. It cannot dwell exclusively on the intrinsic value it achieves for itself without introducing an arbitrary narrowness. Only by transferring its concern to "coordinations wider than personality" can the self affirm the values it is inextricably bound up with. Experience at its widest, its fullest, its deepest, its most adequate, is God's. It is that to which our concern should be directed, not to some future state of our own selfhood.

This line of reasoning is put forth tentatively, for on these questions there can be no final dogmatism. Yet it should be emphasized that this argument does not merely seek to reconcile us with the secularity of contemporary experience which wishes to renounce all other-worldly concerns as distracting wishful thinking. It is governed by a religious concern asking whether subjective immortality is ultimately desirable in the eyes of God. If the prolongation of the self beyond the life of the body is ultimately restrictive, then we should lose it in order to find our lives merged within the life of God. Perhaps in this transfer of concern from our own life to God's we may discover this final Peace.

Prescinding now from questions of immortality and the life of God, what hope can we reasonably have for the overcoming of evil in this finite, temporal world of everyday experience?

The first thing that must be said is that this future is most risky and uncertain. Classical theism, for all the difficulties it might have with present evil, can be serene in the confidence that someday God will wipe out all evil. After all, he is all-powerful, and needs only to assume full control of the world to make it conform to his will. Process theism, by relinquishing the claim that God could completely control the world in order to overcome the problem of present evil, cannot have this traditional assurance about the future. We are faced with an ineluctable dilemma: *Either* God has the power to overcome evil unilaterally, and he should have already, *or* he does not, and we have no guarantee that he will ever be able to. Process theism has chosen to embrace the second horn of this dilemma. God cannot guarantee that evil will be overcome simply because he is not the sole agent determining the outcome of the world. It is a joint enterprise involving a vast multiplicity of actualities responding to his cosmic purposes. Since all these actualities are free to respond as they will, it is conceivable that most may all elect to frustrate the divine aim. The world could possibly generate into near chaos. There can be no metaphysical guarantee against such a catastrophe.

On the other hand, there is a strong pragmatic ground for hoping in God, and that lies in the evolutionary advance of the world during the observable past (that is to say, during the past eighteen billion years or so). Up until now God seems to be able to elicit ever richer forms of complexity from the world, and there is all the reason to expect that he will be able to continue to do this in the future.

This hope, however, need not be especially comforting to the human race. Many, if not most, species have become extinct in the course of this evolutionary advance, and there is good reason to anticipate that this may be our fate as well. Then *we* would be defeated, though not God. The human experiment would have failed, but God could continue on his quest for more intensive forms of existence, if not on this planet, then elsewhere in the universe. Earlier in the history of mankind this danger of extinction was not so evident, but it threatens our generation on every side, particularly in terms of nuclear annihilation or ecological suicide.

In the face of these dangers, can we have any confidence in the power of God to sustain the human enterprise? Here I think we can find renewed meaning in the death and resurrection of Jesus as a profound symbol of hope. If our analysis of Jesus' death is correct, this event signified a defeat for God by the forces of evil, so much so that God was not able to comfort Jesus in the hour of his deepest need on the cross. That experience of despair wrung from Jesus' lips the cry, "My God, my God, why have you forsaken me?" The forces of evil conspired to defeat God, but he was able to triumph over evil in the end by raising up Jesus as the Christ. This resurrection of Christ can be the basis of our hope in God for a human future. The forces of evil could conceivably overwhelm God. Against that there is no metaphysical guarantee. But against such attacks God has hitherto emerged victorious, and what he has already done he can do again. Because we remember Christ's resurrection we can reasonably put our trust and hope in God for our future.

Note that this hope based on the resurrection is quite different from the traditional hope in subjective immortality. Many, following Paul, have argued that if Christ be raised from the dead, we shall be also. The cogency of that argument depends wholly upon the first-century expectation of the general resurrection of the dead in terms of which Paul and the early Christians interpreted their experience of the risen Christ. That expectation also had to interpret Christ's singular resurrection as a preliminary manifestation of the general resurrection very shortly to follow. This keenly anticipated event never took place. Hence we have used a very different framework of interpretation, that of evolutionary emergence, in order to interpret Paul's experience of the risen Christ.

This interpretation of the risen Christ does not rest upon any concept of a disembodied soul. It is precisely because the risen Christ has a body constituted by his disciples that he can live and act. Our interpretation is entirely neutral on the question whether there can be any subjective immortality for us, since the resurrection of Jesus as Christ with his church was such a singular event, and did not necessarily require subjective immortality as generally understood. It is most unfortunate that the question of personal immortality became so inextricably bound up with the question of the resurrection of Christ, because as immortality has become questionable in our age, so has Christ's resurrection. But the two issues stand on very different logical grounds. Whether there be subjective immortality or not is peripheral to the Christian faith. Insofar as resurrection is understood in terms of immortality, it is perhaps an optional belief for the Christian faith. But the resurrection of Christ as the emergence of the church is hardly optional. It is the heart of the New Testament proclamation and the basis for our life in Christ. It may well be also the grounds for our hope in the future of mankind.

NOTES

1. *RM*, pp. 110–11.

2. Charles Hartshorne, "Time, Death, and Everlasting Life," *The Logic of Perfection* (LaSalle, Ill.: Open Court, 1962), pp. 245–62.

3. Schubert Ogden, "The Meaning of Christian Hope," *Union Seminary Quarterly Review* 30 (1975), 153–64.

4. David Griffin, "The Possibility of Subjective Immortality in Whitehead's Philosophy," *The Modern Schoolman* 53/1 (November 1975), 39–57.

5. John Cobb, "What Is the Future? A Process Perspective," in *Hope and the Future of Man*, ed. Ewert H. Cousins (Philadelphia: Fortress Press, 1972), pp. 1–14.

6. Marjorie Suchocki, "The Question of Immortality," *Journal of Religion* 57/3 (July 1977), 288–306. See also our joint essay on "A Whiteheadian Reflection on Subjective Immortality" in *Process Studies* 7/1 (Spring 1977), 1–13, showing that the way God experiences through me (by means of the subjective form of my satisfaction) may be the same as my experiencing in God.

7. *AI*, p. 267.

8. The technical details of this proposal need to be worked out in terms of Whitehead's principles. This may prove to be impossible, for they seem to require a direct objectification of God's temporal experience which, unlike his nontemporal experience and the experience of actual occasions, never reaches the completion required for objectification.

9. *PR*, p. 525.

10. *Ibid.*, italics added.

11. Cf. *Ibid.*, p. 47.

12. *Ibid.*, p. 532.

13. See A. H. Johnson's report, "Whitehead as Teacher and Philosopher," *Philosophy and Phenomenological Research* 29 (1968–69), 373.

14. *AI*, p. 367.

15. *Ibid.*

16. *Ibid.*, p. 368.

Epilogue

Since the impetus for process theism has primarily come from the philosophies of Whitehead and Hartshorne, it is not surprising that most process theology heretofore has been largely preoccupied with the problems and questions they have left us. It is time, however, we fleshed out the thinness of these philosophical abstractions with the concreteness of the biblical witness to God's interaction with Israel and with the church. For process theism recognizes both the necessary and the contingent aspects of God. Philosophy properly and adequately analyzes God's necessary aspects, but cannot tell us what his contingent aspects are, other than the bare assertion that there *are* such contingent aspects, features of God's activity which happen to be so but just as well could have been otherwise. The Bible's insistence upon historical and geographical particularity (e.g., Abraham, Israel, Zion), often an embarrassment to theological universality, has marked it out as the primary source for man's witness to the involvement of God in history. The radical contingency of this involvement, known to us through the Scriptures, thus precisely complements the abstract conceptuality process theism offers, while this conceptuality in turn illumines the way in which we today can appropriate this rich heritage.

If this common history of God and man is truly contingent, then man's free response is an essential element in the story. This in turn undercuts the traditional assumption that God controls the future (or at least knows it in detail), and has everything already planned out (chapter 2). God's power is persuasive, not controlling. His is the power of the future operative in the present, providing those possibilities which, if fully actualized in our creaturely response, will bring about the achievement of the good.

This is the power of divine lure, expressed in the vision of the future reigning of God (chapter 3).

This divine persuasion reached a critical point of intensity in the event of Jesus, where through his life, death, and resurrection a new level in the creation of the world was achieved, the transhuman reality of the living body of Christ (chapter 5). "Christ" for us is not simply identical with the Logos, the second member of the Trinity, which is the totality of the rational features of God available for (partial) actualization in the world. Christ is that divine Word effectively addressed to the human condition. Since our existence and condition are radically contingent, so is that divine address, which can only be discovered through revelation (chapter 4). That contingent divine address may be variously understood, but we have interpreted it in terms of the emergent body of Christ.

In speaking of Jesus' resurrection in terms of the body of Christ, we mean to steer a middle course between two opposite extremes. On the one hand, we wish to challenge the implicit individualism inherent in the traditional understanding of the Risen Christ as a separate individual existing apart from his Christian followers, either in some resuscitated form during those forty days Luke speaks of (Acts 1:3) or as assimilated within the Godhead. On the other hand, we do not wish to be misunderstood as claiming that the Risen Christ is merely the collective spirit of the church, as if it were just the dynamism achieved through the merging of many humans in a common task. The analogy of a living animal organism might be helpful here. The collective spirit of the church would be like the common life of the body, which is simply the merging of the vitalities of the individual cells. It could perhaps be enough to explain the activity of the body, were it only sleeping. But when it is awake and alert, any animal body is coordinated in its activity by its mind. To be sure, this mind may not exist apart from its body, but neither can the body fully act as an alert living organism apart from the mind. The Risen Christ is just such a mind for his body. And just as the higher forms of mind enjoy consciousness, we should expect that the mind of this transhuman reality enjoys an even more intense form of consciousness of its own, distinct from temporal humans. It is also distinct from God's consciousness, for there was a time, namely, at the resurrection, when this consciousness came to be.

Jesus' death bears ultimate significance for us because of the resurrection. Without that stamp of divine approval, his death would have been another of the deaths of the martyrs. But the death of God's chosen One reveals the depths of anguish and suffering of God at the hands of creaturely evil, for he has pledged to accept the unacceptable, even at such cost. The cross also marks the defeat of God, momentarily stymied from effecting his purposes, but the resurrection shows that God is able to triumph over such defeat (chapter 6). This, as we have just seen in the preceding chapter, is our ultimate basis for hope in the future course of the world under God.

The Christian community's concern for the role of Christ within a strictly monotheistic economy gave rise to the traditional problem of the Trinity. Since we conceive of the Risen Christ with his body as a level of reality distinct from both God and man, our solution is closer to Paul's original subordinationism (God-Christ-Spirit) than to the eventual coordinationism (Father-Son-Spirit) adopted at Nicaea. Yet the doctrine of the Trinity also expresses some speculative insights most congenial to Christian philosophy which process theism can appropriate (chapter 7). The classical description of the Father begetting the Son before all worlds can also describe the way in which God, in the Whiteheadian conceptuality, creates himself by envisaging all the pure forms as constituting the metaphysical order God and the world exemplify. Moreover, the Logos (=Son) and the Spirit are closely correlated with the two natures of God whereby he exemplifies that order, the primordial and the consequent natures.

Besides all this, the specific relation between the Father and the Logos is most important in safeguarding two truths, often obscured in theology's ongoing dialogue with philosophy:

(1) God does not simply transcend all rational structures whatsoever, but stands revealed in the Logos. This insures that philosophical analysis of the nature of God is both possible and proper. As we have seen, such knowledge is not sufficient for it cannot speak effectively to our human contingent condition, but this does not mean that in its own sphere it is not necessary and valid.

This stricture is often honored in its breach, as in mysticism, Neoplatonism, the negative theology of the early Greek fathers, or in the contemporary insistence by Tillich that the divine being-itself is beyond all beings. All such formulations implicitly elevate God the Father (or the underlying divine substance) to a higher ultimacy than the other members of the Trinity, and then treat this element as really God. If the Trinity is not to be understood tritheistically, the generation of the Logos from the Father is God's self-expression, whereby God's nature is articulated in ways at least partially accessible to discursive reason.

(2) On the other hand, God is not subject to some uncreated metaphysical structure. There is no ultimate pattern of being, independently discoverable by reason, to which he must conform. Such a thesis was carried to its extreme by Leibniz, who argued that God must choose the best of the compossible worlds. These compossibilities could be ranked quite independently of God's choosing, and he had only to call the one ranked best into being. In contrast, Whitehead asserts that God both "exemplifies and establishes the categoreal conditions."[1] He is their ultimate source. They receive their value for his valuing, not vice versa.

This is very much in accord with the ancient Hebrew understanding of God's name: "I am who I am" (Ex. 3:14). Thomas Aquinas took this to mean that God is pure being, being-itself, but that interpretation ignores the role of the reiterated first person singular. This phrase, combining an open-ended imperfect verb (in either the active or causative mood) with a highly indefinite relative pronoun, can be interpreted in a great many different ways. I regard as basic the proclamation of sovereign freedom: "I will be what I will be," fashioned analogously to the words: "I will be gracious to whom I will be gracious, and will show mercy on whom I will show mercy" (Ex. 33:19).

According to this reading it is all too easy to conclude that the original Hebraic understanding claimed God was radically without any nature, radically free to constitute himself anew in any moment. Such an existentialist interpretation violates our first stricture that God stands revealed in the rational structure of the Logos. It also ignores the counterbalancing factor present in the ancient Hebraic view, namely, that this sovereign Lord freely enters into covenants with men, with Noah, with Abraham, and with the whole house of Israel assembled at Sinai. Also, this Lord is faithful to his promises. In this historical and political context, the promises of God provide that sort of ultimate stability later sought in metaphysics.

In a human life this combination of freedom and faithfulness is praiseworthy for the integrity it achieves. Human integrity should be judged by two criteria: (1) the steadfastness of character it expresses, and (2) the values chosen as the basis for that integrity, for they must be sufficiently inclusive in order to serve as a satisfactory guide for the resolution of all particular crises. Such integrity can only be manifested in a temporal series of free decisions because we never confront the totality of those situations comprising our lives all at once. We choose our values hopefully, tentatively, awaiting future developments to see whether we can afford to reaffirm them. A complete restructuring of values, such as the "radical conversion" Sartre envisions, is always possible, for we may well discover that the values we have lived by are inadequate as guides for handling present crises. In that case Sartre's strictures against inauthenticity are quite pertinent. It will not do to reaffirm the old values mechanically, despite present need. We must then have the courage to tear down and reshape our structure of values. A deeper integrity might thereby arise, since we may find ourselves embodying richer and more inclusive values. Nevertheless a break has occurred. The original integrity has been judged and found wanting. Human integrity cannot thus be an inherent quality, given at the outset, but an achievement only tentatively and gradually achieved. We can never know how well it is achieved until we can review a man's total life.

The biblical drama is the biography of God, whereby the integrity of his values are gradually made manifest in the vicissitudes of the concrete situations of Israel, Jesus, and the church. These values in all of their complex richness cannot be simply given at the outset; they must be temporally emergent as layer upon layer is added to the account of God's dealings with man. The concrete character of each situation needs to be explored.

Nevertheless there is a profound difference between divine and human integrity. In addition, to confront each situation immediately at hand, and to bring it to a definite conclusion, God has the task of ordering all conceivable possibilities. This cosmic ordering cannot be simply temporal, for in that case we face two equally unacceptable alternatives: (1) Suppose God changes his ordering from time to time, according to which possibilities are judged to be better or worse. Then what was better now becomes worse, and vice versa. Given God's first ordering, no other ordering can be justified. Or, given some later ordering, no earlier one can be justified. With different orderings values would become totally arbitrary, relative not merely to changing circumstance or cultural milieu, or to different individuals, but also to the passing whims of a cosmic ruler. (2) Suppose, to avoid these evils, we conceive God's first temporal decision to be perfect and complete. It could not be tentative and incomplete, for then it would be subject to the uncertainty that it might prove to be inadequate in some later situation. This would pack all of God's decision-making back into some first temporal moment, a very problematic notion in itself. Then all God's decisions from that moment on would merely be mechanical reaffirmations of that original choice.

What is needed is an openness and tentativeness allowing for the ongoing exercise of divine freedom coupled with an underlying integrity which cannot possibly be threatened by whatever happens. This we find in Whitehead's conception of the primordial envisagement of all pure possibilities. This one, ultimate decision is basically nontemporal, whereby all the possibilities are ordered, and God determines himself to be the sort of God he is. It is thereby God's act of self-creation. Or, to express it in classical terms, it is the way the Father (=the originating power) generates the Son (=the Logos, the order of all possibility) "before all worlds" (=nontemporally). This basically nontemporal ordering is then temporally emergent in God's interaction with the world. It is never fully given in any temporal moment.

Thus while the nature of God is ultimately derived from a divine decision, it is not a merely temporal decision. This then qualifies the thrust of that declaration, "I will be what I will be." While God may respond differently to differing circumstances, there is an underlying consistency of character and value that is open to philosophical examination. While process theism welcomes expressions of God's dynamic activity, I for one am hesitant ever to endorse any change in God's values not dictated by a change in the objective situation. Yet God is portrayed as not having determined the wickedness of Sodom and Gomorrah prior to his consultation with Abraham (Gen. 18:21), and Moses successfully averts God's original intention to destroy the Israelites, although Israel's idolatry with the golden calf remains just what it was before Moses' intercession (Ex. 32:7–14).[2]

The biblical writers have not been particularly sensitive to the demand for an underlying consistency of character among the differing portrayals of God. Various scholars have noticed and emphasized the resulting incompatibilities. John L. McKenzie has written:

We simply do not believe in the Great Warrior who exterminated the Canaanites. Some who shared our faith did. They also professed belief in Jesus Christ the Son of God who said that he who would save his life must lose it, and who implied that a good way to lose it quickly is to love those who hate you and pray for those who persecute you. How does one speak of a god who exhibits both these features? I am compelled to say simply he does not exist, and that those who professed this monstrous faith worshipped an idol.[3]

These logical inconsistencies, which so trouble us today because of the implicit way in which we have accepted the perspective of Greek rationality, did not concern the biblical thinkers. Even after we have been admonished to love our enemies and to ''be perfect, as your heavenly Father is perfect'' (Matt. 5:44, 48), Paul can quote with approval the divine decision: ''Jacob I loved, but Esau I hated'' (Rom. 9:13, quoting from Mal. 1:2–3). It is a logical contradiction for God to love all men, including his enemies, and yet also hate Esau, but this does not seem to bother Paul at all. For there is an inconsistency only if we introduce the philsopher's assumption that God has an unchanging nature, such that the way we now experience divine activity must also characterize God's activity in the past. Paul's understanding of God, however, was primarily historical. He apprehended God in terms of his present activity, as presently understood, but also accepted without challenge the authoritative witness to divine activity in the past. In appealing to this rejection of Esau, Paul was not arguing that the chosenness of Jacob must require the rejection of Esau, let alone trying to justify any hatred for the Edomites. He was simply trying to justify his present understanding of God, involving as it did notions of election and predestination, and for this purpose the authoritative word of the tradition was sufficient. He does not inquire whether the interpretive patterns employed by the historical witness were the same as his own, or even compatible with them. This is a modern preoccupation, growing out of our concern with universality.

It may be precisely this lack of concern for temporal consistency which makes it possible for biblical literature to give us such a rich account of the activity of God. It allows for the accumulation of many different perspectives, each roughly consistent within itself but not necessarily with the others. Had a strict demand for consistency among these various perspectives been present, no new understanding of God could have emerged without a repudiation of the old. Given the conservative nature of religious practice, it is more than likely that the old view would have won out every time, stifling all new creative imagination. The genius of the Hebrew imagination was that it was able to accept and affirm the witness to God's former acts, even as understood from an older perspective, while at the same time proclaiming what God was about to do as grasped from a newer standpoint. Moreover, it was precisely the acceptance of the old which provided a rich matrix for present creative imagination to reach new levels of insight. This combination of the old and the new was experienced as a living reality, for God, having graciously acted on behalf of Israel, was now prepared to do a new thing.

The danger of a premature demand for consistency may be seen in the Greek experience. Here heightened moral sensitivity was not handled historically, but became part of philosophy's general criticism of its inherited myth. The notion that it is most appropriate for the divine to be unchanging enters the philosophical tradition very early. If Aristotle's report carries over the words of Anaximander (and not merely some later inference), Anaximander, himself already so conceived his basic principle, the *apeiron* (the indefinite): "And this, they say, is the divine. For it is immortal and indestructible, as Anaximander and most of the natural philosophers maintain."[4] At any rate, Xenophanes emphatically claims that God:

> ... ever abides
> In the selfsame place without moving; nor is it fitting
> For him to move hither and thither, changing his place.[5]

The result of this conception of the divine was devastating. With one blow the Olympian gods were consigned to oblivion. How could there be strife or any sort of interaction among the gods if only the unchanging could really be perfect? Xenophanes seems to have had a fierce belief in his one divine being, but it seems to have been too vague to capture the imagination of his compatriots. They were only too aware of the incisiveness of his critique against the Homeric deities, and in fact the Greeks gradually lost faith in these gods during the ensuing century. Greek philosophy sought to conceive some underlying divinity which Zeus, Hermes, Aphrodite, and the rest all participated in, but in the process lost the personality of God, and with it all popular allegiance. Faced with the many gods of antiquity, the biblical tradition took an approach that was wiser. It did not initially insist upon their nonexistence. The injunction was clear and practical: "Thou shalt have no other gods before me." This is primarily a vow of fidelity, with no necessary theoretical implications. If in marriage a man and woman take each other, forswearing all others, this by no means implies they are the only ones in existence. Yet the eventual outcome of the biblical experience, initially elevating one God above all competing powers, was the discovery that these gods were no gods at all. Thus monotheism can grow out of an earlier henotheism, with apparently little awareness of the diverse theological views of the differing historical layers.

In the course of many centuries the biblical record has left us with an impressive compendium of historical testimony to God's dealings with Israel, expressed in terms of a wide variety of diverse and often conflicting perspectives, which so perplexed the Greek mind as it tried to come to terms with the foundations of Christian theology. No wonder it so often sought refuge in allegory! Many biblical theologians are suspicious of the use the church has made of philosophy in understanding this heritage, yet even they accept the demand for philsophical consistency. And it is precisely this demand which shatters the thought-world of the biblical writers themselves. For now it becomes no longer possible to incorporate other perspectives within one's own simply because they authoritatively witness to God's past actions. We must now show how the total range of testimony can be accommodated, more or less, within a single, consistent perspective. This requirement brings us to philosophy, for it is the one discipline best suited for the construction of such all-embracing concepts.

History has served the cause of God well. In no other culture or span of time has man's understanding of God's ways progressed so much as in ancient Israel. At the time of the Judges, Yahweh was conceived as simply one of the various tribal deities, along with Molech of Moab and Chemosh of Ammon (see Judg. 11:24), yet barely six centuries later Second Isaiah can proclaim with monotheistic fervor the glories of the Lord as creator of the world and redeemer of Israel. Nothing in the history of Christian doctrine since the New Testament, certainly not since Nicaea, can rival this for growth in increased sensitivity. In the light of this it is very tempting to want to continue to exploit the paradigm of historical interpretation for our understanding of God today. Unfortunately it is a paradigm that has outlived its usefulness, for at least two reasons:

(1) The book of Job now stands in its way as a massive roadblock. The

righteous are not always rewarded, nor the wicked punished. This observation was already causing concern to the thoughtful during the last years of Judah's monarchy. According to the historian of Kings, Manasseh was one of the worst kings to sit on the throne of Judah, and Josiah one of the very best. Yet Manasseh has a long and peaceful reign of some fifty-five years, and Josiah is cut down in battle before he was yet forty, despite Huldah's word from the Lord that he would die in peace (2 Kings 22:20; cf. 23:29). Jeremiah and Habakkuk questioned the justice of God, as did many of those exiled in Babylon. Why should they be required to pay for the sins of their forefathers, particularly in the light of the emerging realization that each man should be answerable for his own sins? (Jer. 31:27–30; Ezek. 18:1–4). The author of the book of Job faced this question squarely,[6] and resolved it as best he could dramatically, but no resolution is really possible, given the presuppositions of the time.

It is a commonplace to observe that Job undercuts the easy assumptions of the wisdom school or of the Deuteronomic historian. It is not equally realized that it undercuts the basis for the whole prophetic interpretation of history. Amos and Hosea could threaten doom upon Israel in the confidence that this was God's just punishment for its sin. If in fact there is no correlation between conduct and consequence, the nerve of this sort of interpretation of history is severed.

We seek to understand God as purely persuasive. But what if this persuasion proves ineffective, because the people are recalcitrant? The king can compel obedience by punishing the rebellious, and this same model was transferred to God. But, as we have seen, any such coercive measures depend upon creaturely agencies partially beyond God's control. The gap between the "ought" and the "is" applies equally well to any theory of rewards and punishments. Measures which, if directly controlled by God, should be interpreted as instances of God's wrath may not have been so intended. Thus it is possible that Huldah's prophecy concerning Josiah properly reflected the aims of God, in this case frustrated by Pharaoh Necho and the king's own miscalculation as to the probable consequences of that confrontation between Egypt and Israel.

According to the law of the prophet, if the word spoken in the name of the Lord does not come to pass, then the prophet has spoken falsely (Deut. 18:22). But that law presupposes that God directly controls man's destiny, to insure that his threats or promises would be carried out. Yet, even at the time, Israel understood prophecy as the open-ended proclamation of divine intent, modifiable in terms of its response. This is the point of the story of Jonah, and Jeremiah had a lively sense of its truth (see, e.g., Jer. 26:3, or 18:1–11). The non-fulfillment of Micah's prophecy against the temple was understood in Jeremiah's time as the result of Hezekiah's repentance (Jer. 26:16–19). Perhaps we should evaluate the truth or falsity of prophecy in terms of whether it correctly reflects God's intentions in that particular situation, not how it was in fact carried out. In that case Jeremiah's prediction of a bad end for Jehoiakim (Jer. 22:19; 36:30–31), while it was apparently never fulfilled, nevertheless remains authentic prophetic declaration. As I read them, both Isaiah and Micah fully expected the destruction of Jerusalem and Judah at the hands of Sennacherib,[7] and by their lights this is what ought to have happened. This may be truer prophecy than the later legendary accretions in which Isaiah predicts the Lord's miraculous deliverance of the city of Jerusalem from the Assyrian siege (Isa. 36–37), even though that reinterpretation of the prophet's role may have saved the book of Isaiah for the canon.

Most of the prophetic writings we now have are clustered around three major crises in Israel's history: (1) the fall of Samaria in 722 B.C., (2) the invasion by Sennacherib in 701 B.C., and (3) the fall of Jerusalem in 586 B.C. In the case of the first and third instances, these events could be truly interpreted as the execution of God's wrath. Thus the prophetic declaration of divine intent based on what ought to be the case could coincide with fulfilled prediction. If in hindsight Israel collected only those prophecies which could be understood as properly fulfilled prediction, in accordance with the Deuteronomic law of the prophet, there is no way of determining how many other "true" prophets there may have been, "true" in the sense that they accurately proclaimed the character of God's intent.

(2) The prophetic interpretation of history was plausible when only Israel and its Lord were the protagonists, and the other nations were simply onlookers or instrumentalities of God's will. When the horizon is widened to embrace all the nations, God's will has to be reconceived from their standpoint as well. In the Exodus traditions the Israelites could enjoy a good fight with Egypt, since this conflict was regarded as simply the means whereby God redeemed them out of the house of bondage. But what is God's purpose vis-à-vis the Egyptians? The status of God's in-

strumentalities becomes even more enigmatic, because it is only the arrogance, greed, and aggressiveness of the Assyrians and the Babylonians which make them unconscious tools for God's punishment. Habakkuk protests: "Why dost thou look on faithless men, and art silent when the wicked swallows up the man more righteous then he?" (1:13). Jeremiah can only proclaim God's judgment against *all* the nations at the hands of Babylon, and then Babylon is to be judged in turn (25:8–14).

Thus in the end, the apocalyptic writers who use the horizon of universal history have recourse to angelic instrumentalities of God's will. Angels can directly and unambiguously accomplish the divine purpose, for in theory they lack the creaturely freedom that so distorts the course of history. Yet, in doing so, the presupposition underlying divine persuasion is destroyed.

If Whitehead is right that "God's purpose in the creative advance is the evocation of intensities"[8] for each creature or group as it arises, and that history must be conceived "as the theatre of diverse groups of idealists respectively urging ideals incompatible for conjoint realization,"[9] then perhaps we should see God as encouraging each to pursue the good it envisages, despite the conflict this may entail. (To be sure, compromise and the harmonization of interests may well be among the goods the parties are also enjoined to pursue.) The complexity and diversity of interests and values represented in universal history, coupled with the radical uncertainty about any connection between performance and deserts, make it impossible today to discern God's providential hand in it with the confidence of Israel's prophets.

The prophetic corpus of the Old Testament oversimplifies history in two directions. It sees a direct correlation between conduct and consequence, and it concentrates its attention narrowly on Israel. It cannot do justice to the complexities of universal history. Yet this was a most important oversimplification, for it made possible for the Jews to accept their fate as the just punishment of God, and to accept the Torah as the book by which they would live. Without that credibility of the prophetic oversimplification, the exiled Jews might have lost their identity as the people of God. Israel might have vanished before the Christ of Israel could appear.

If for no other reason, the universality of the Christian proclamation of salvation for all requires that the particularity of historical categories be replaced by the universality of philosophical concepts. But it is important that there be no premature abandonment of history's nurturing role, as the fate of Greek religious sensibility indicates. Had the question of a monarchy in Israel been addressed in the absolutistic terms of political philosophy, the result could very well have been disastrous. On the one hand, if the Israelite monarchy were seen as essential, then the whole foundation of Israel would have collapsed when Jerusalem was taken by Nebuchadnezzar. On the other hand, if the monarchy were understood as inimical to true theism, Israel at the time of Samuel and Saul might have succumbed to the Philistines. Without a royal theology, it is difficult to imagine how the anticipation of a future king could have arisen. Jesus' own role, at least in the eyes of his disciples and the later church, would have had less justification without this rich matrix of messianic expectation.

History provides the proper way into theology, but philosophy is the critic of the consistency of its perspectives. Theology today must be articulated by means of philosophical concepts, and these should be evaluated according to purely philosophical criteria of consistency, coherence, adequacy, and applicability. Yet if these concepts are to be adequate and applicable to all experience, this experience must also include the experience of biblical man. While philosophy may judge the consistency of his interpretive standpoints, it cannot gainsay his witness to the contingencies of divine action.

Process theism is the natural ally of biblical history, for process is history abstractly conceived. Process theism can provide the contemporary conceptuality by which we can appropriate this ancient literature, while the biblical tradition can provide those concrete particularities whereby our lives are given final meaning.

NOTES

1. PR, p. 522.
2. For an incisive analysis of this last incident, see George W. Coats, "The King's Loyal Opposition: Obedience and Authority in Exodus 32–34," pp. 91–109 in *Canon and Authority: Essays in Old Testament and Theology,* ed. George W. Coats and Burke O. Long (Philadelphia: Fortress, 1977).
3. John L. McKenzie, "Biblical Anthropomorphism and the Humaneness of God," p. 182 in *Religion and the Humanizing of Man,* ed. James M. Robinson (Waterloo, Ontario: Council on the Study of Religion, 1972).

4. Aristotle, Physics iii.4, about 203ᵇ12. See Werner Jaeger's discussion of this passage in *The Theology of the Early Greek Philosophers* (New York: Oxford University Press, 1947), p. 25.

5. Xenophanes, B26, in Herman Diels, *DieFragmente der Vorsokratiker,* ed. Walther Kranz, 5th ed. (Berlin: Weidmann, 1934–35).

6. I take Job 3–42:6 to be an exilic composition inserted in a traditional folktale which now frames the encounter of Job with his three friends and with God.

7. For Isaiah, Isa. 29:1–4 is the key passage. I take verses 5–8 to be a later reinterpretation by another hand, based upon the ambiguity of the preposition in v. 3, which can be interpreted either as "against" or as "upon."

8. PR, p. 161.

9. AI, p. 356–57.

Index of
Biblical References

Index of
Proper Names

General Index